FLORIDA DAY TRIPS

MIKE MILLER

DEDICATION

To Yadira Cepero, for being my support and inspiration.

ACKNOWLEDGMENTS

I would like to thank Linda, Suzy, Jim, Lee, Cherie, Jean, Robin, and other friends and family for all the miles they wandered around Florida with me, discovering new places and things to do.

Safety Note Florida is home to a variety of potentially dangerous animals, including venomous snakes and scorpions, as well as natural hazards, such as temperature extremes, sudden flash floods, and treacherous tides and currents. Always heed posted safety warnings, take common-sense safety precautions, and remain aware of your surroundings. You're responsible for your own safety.

Editors: Andrew Mollenkof and Geoffrey Wright
Cover and book design: Hilary Harkness
Proofreader: Emily Beaumont
Typography: Karla Linder
Maps: Steve Jones
Indexer: Potomac Indexing, LLC
Front cover photos: Everglades National Park: GagliardiPhotography/shutterstock.com; asphalt: Irina Gutyryak/shutterstock.com; space shuttle: VectorHight/shutterstock.com
Back cover photos: baby turtle: Andre-Johnson/shutterstock.com; Saturn rocket: Wirestock Creators/shutterstock
Photo credits on page 145
ADK branding background on page 148 by chyworks/Shutterstock.com

10 9 8 7 6 5 4 3 2 1
Florida Day Trips by Theme
First Edition 2020, Second Edition 2026

Published by Adventure Publications
An imprint of AdventureKEEN
310 Garfield Street South
Cambridge, Minnesota 55008
(800) 678-7006
adventurepublications.net

Printed in China
Library of Congress Control Number: 2025945434
ISBN 978-1-64755-559-7 (pbk.); 978-1-64755-560-3 (ebook)

FLORIDA DAY TRIPS

MIKE MILLER

MAP 1

WEST FLORIDA, FLORIDA PANHANDLE, BRADENTON, TAMPA AREA

CONTENTS

MAP 1 MAP 2 MAP 3 MAP 4

MAP 2

EAST FLORIDA AND KEY WEST AREA

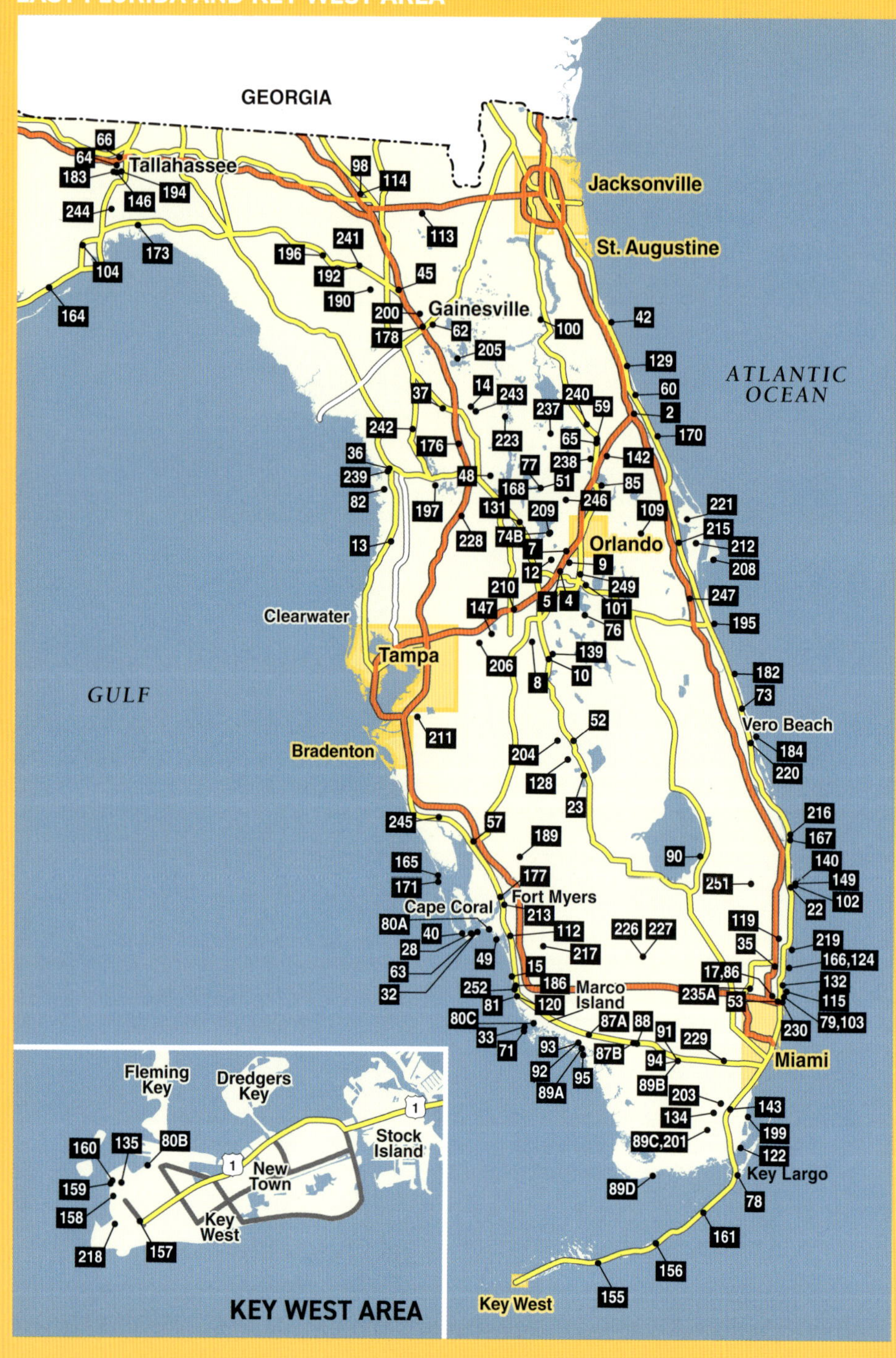

CONTENTS

■ MAP 1 ■ MAP 2 ■ MAP 3 ■ MAP 4

MAP 3

MIAMI AREA

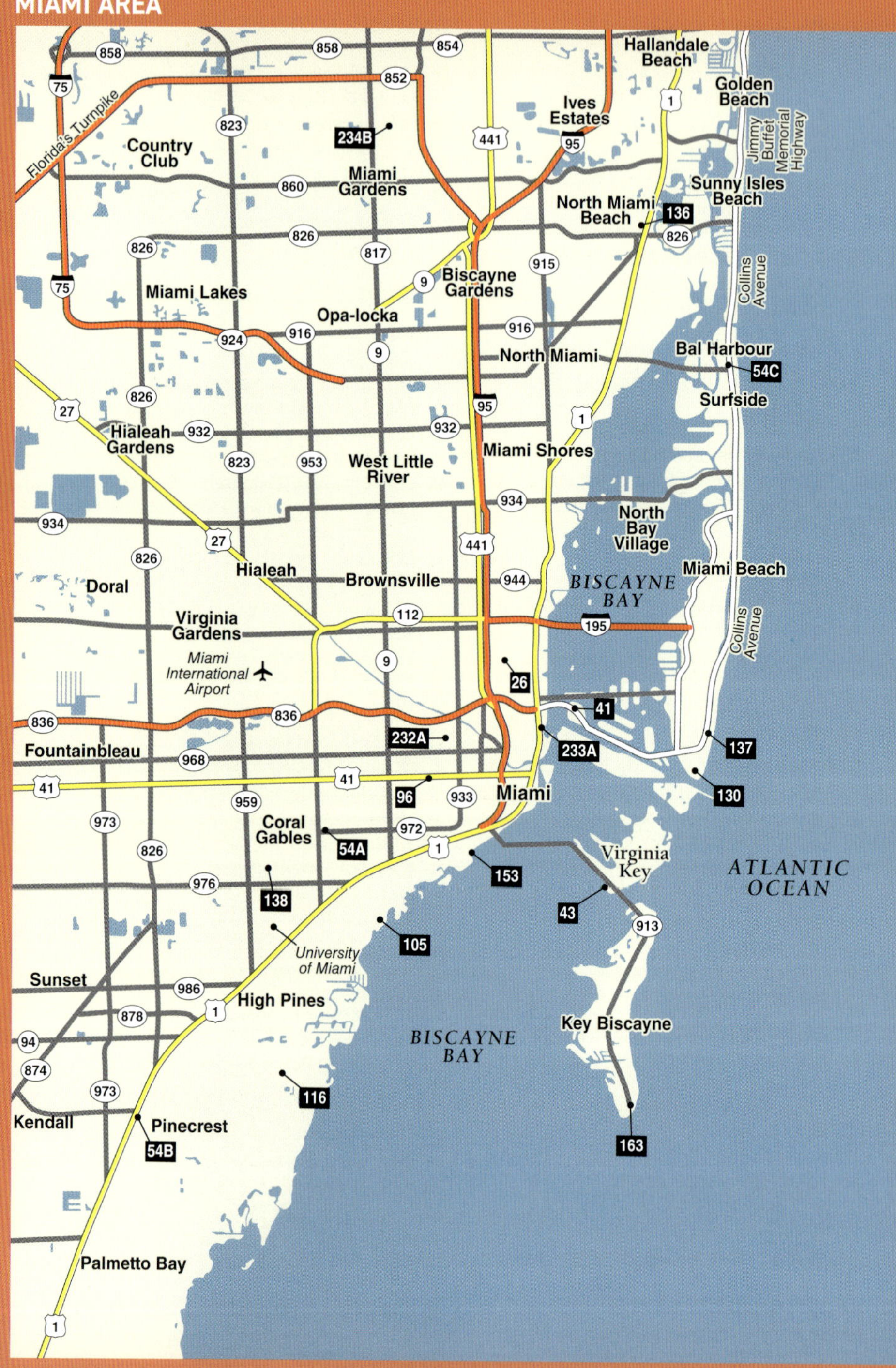

CONTENTS

MAP 1 MAP 2 MAP 3 MAP 4

MAP 4

ST. AUGUSTINE, JACKSONVILLE, AND ORLANDO AREAS

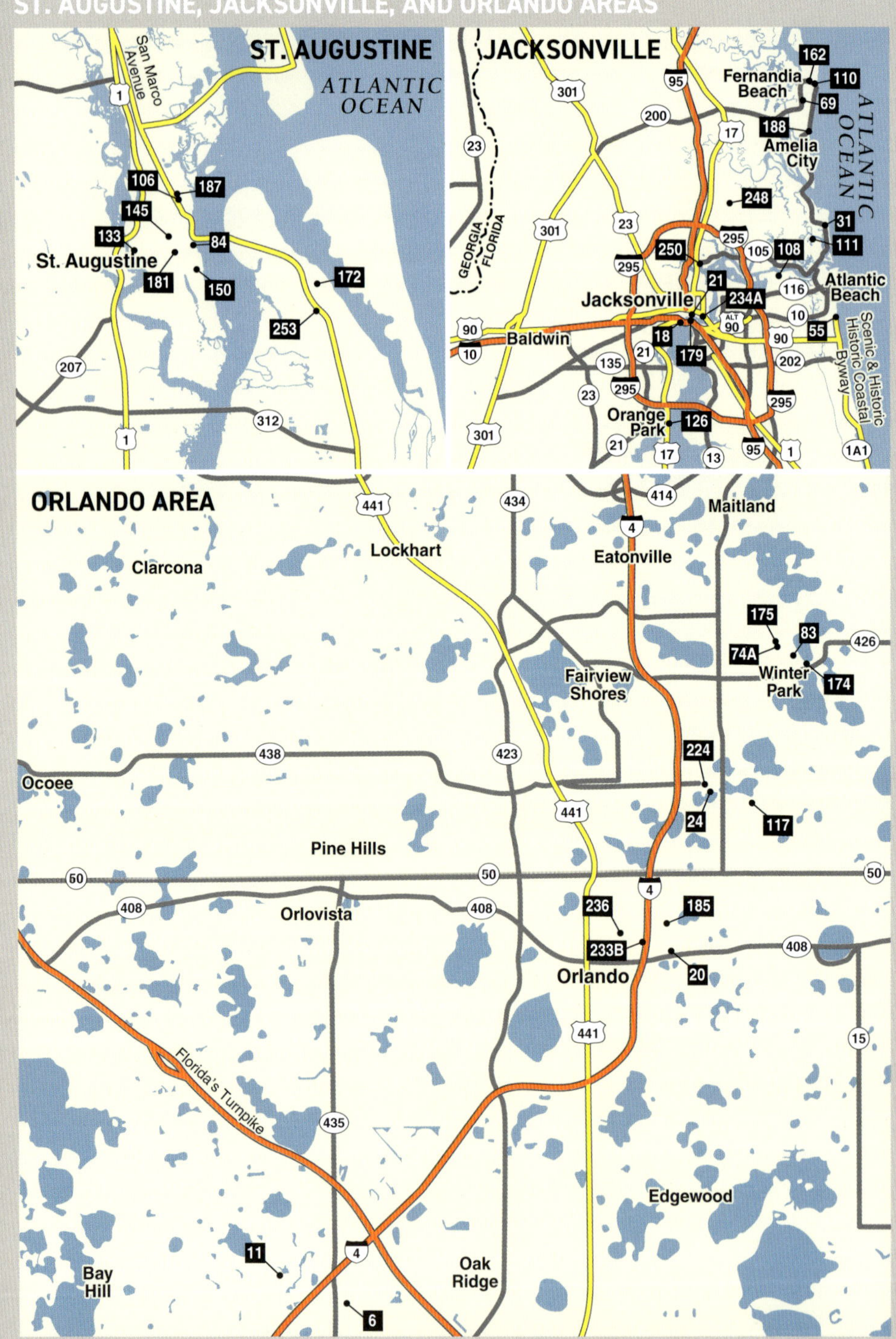

CONTENTS

■ MAP 1 ■ MAP 2 ■ MAP 3 ■ MAP 4

DIVING AT GINNIE SPRINGS, HIGH SPRINGS

CAPE FLORIDA LIGHT, KEY BISCAYNE

FRUIT & SPICE PARK, HOMESTEAD

ANHINGA AT THE VENICE AUDUBON ROOKERY

INTRODUCTION

Florida is one of the greatest states in America for a day trip. As the third-most-populous state, with 23 million people, no spot is more than 60 miles from a beach—a perfect escape for a quick getaway. The Sunshine State's nickname rings true, drawing millions of new visitors annually.

Indigenous people, the earliest humans in Florida, arrived around 14,000 years ago, leaving behind archaeological sites perfect for day-trip exploration. You can visit the Crystal River Archaeological State Park for a glimpse into ancient mound-building cultures.

The Spanish held Florida for over 250 years, split into two periods, and their legacy still shines. Founded in 1565, St. Augustine, the "Ancient City," is America's oldest city and a top day-trip spot for millions. Explore the Castillo de San Marcos National Monument, a 17th-century fortress, for a dose of living history.

Post–Civil War settlers from Southern states pioneered the cattle and citrus industries. They became known as Florida Crackers because of the sound their cattle whips made. Try a citrus grove tour in Lake Wales or a horseback ride at a historic ranch near Okeechobee.

Most of Florida's population lives along the coasts, but the central region boasts quiet towns, rural roads, and attractions ideal for a spontaneous adventure. Check out Mount Dora's quaint shops or DeLand's vibrant murals for a small-town vibe.

Florida has been a pioneer in the aerospace industry since 1950, with the first rocket launch from Cape Canaveral Space Force Station. Kennedy Space Center is the site of many rocket launches, including the historic 1969 round-trip to the moon.

Nature lovers can't miss Florida's state parks, like Blue Spring State Park, where manatees gather in winter, or the Everglades, where visitors can ride airboats through untamed wilderness. Whether you crave history, nature, or a laid-back drive, Florida delivers.

THE WHEEL AT ICON PARK, ORLANDO

From water parks to roller coasters to giant Ferris wheels, you can find fun in Florida.

Does your perfect day include a family visit to a giant theme park, or would you rather go to a smaller, less-expensive attraction? No matter your preference, there are hundreds, if not thousands, of entertaining getaways in Florida. Orlando and central Florida are home to some of the largest, most-famous theme parks in the world, and smaller attractions are scattered across the state.

Welcome to AMUSEMENT & THEME PARKS

In addition to the big theme parks like Walt Disney World Resort, Florida has many smaller attractions, some dating to the 1930s.

LIVE "MERMAIDS" PERFORM IN A NATURAL SPRING AT THE HISTORIC WEEKI WACHEE SPRINGS STATE PARK, OPENED IN 1947, SPRING HILL

Find out more about AMUSEMENT & THEME PARKS

1 BUSCH GARDENS

10165 North McKinley Drive
Tampa, FL 33612; 813-884-4386
buschgardens.com/tampa

You will never get bored at Busch Gardens in Tampa. It is a 335-acre animal-themed park that contains nine roller coasters, two water rides, plus other rides and animal attractions. The park is also adjacent to a sister water park, Adventure Island. Busch Gardens has several themed areas and attractions, such as Morocco, Congo, Nairobi, Edge of Africa, and Egypt. Some are walk-through exhibits where you can observe animals in their natural habitat. Bird Gardens is a free-flight aviary where more than 500 tropical birds from all over the world make their homes. You can also hand-feed a kangaroo and see crocodiles, meerkats, lions, hyenas, and hippos.

2 DAYTONA INTERNATIONAL SPEEDWAY

1801 West International Speedway Boulevard
Daytona Beach, FL 3211;
800-748-7467
daytonainternationalspeedway.com

This famous racetrack features several events during the year, such as the Daytona 500, the Rolex 24, and many more. If you are in Daytona at times other than race days, the speedway offers tours on a first-come, first-served basis. Drive through the main entrance and follow the signs to the tours. There are three basic tour types: Speedway, All-Access, and VIP. The tours range in time from 30 minutes for the Speedway to 90 minutes for the All-Access, and 3 hours for the VIP. Prices increase as tour time increases. These are tram tours, and after the tour you can visit the Motorsports Hall of Fame of America. You will see all kinds of stock cars, sports cars, and motorcycles.

3 DINOSAUR WORLD

5145 Harvey Tew Road
Plant City, FL 33565; 813-717-9865
dinosaurworld.com/florida

Nobody seems to know for sure why kids are so crazy about dinosaurs, but a visit to this place will convince you they are. You will have a chance to wander around hundreds of replicas of the giant reptiles, displayed in their true size. Tyrannosaurus rex is there, of course, along with even scarier creatures you might never have heard of. You can uncover a 27-foot dinosaur skeleton at the Bone Yard and pretend you are a paleontologist at the Fossil Dig. The Exploration Cave Show lets you interact with a paleontologist on a tour through a cave, a dig site, and a workstation. There is also a separate museum, a gift shop, and a playground, as well as plenty of free parking.

4 DISNEY SPRINGS

1486 East Buena Vista Drive
Orlando, FL 32830; 407-939-6244
disneysprings.com

You will have no trouble at all spending an enjoyable day or two at Disney Springs, an outdoor shopping, dining, and entertainment complex at Walt Disney World Resort. The original complex opened in 1975 and has been expanded and renamed over the years. Disney Springs has a fictional history that says it was settled in the 1800s by a cattle rancher. The complex has four separately themed areas, each reflecting a different time in the fictional history of the town. Each area has an architectural style typical of its period. Admission is free. Buses and water taxis operated by Disney Transport provide transportation between Disney Springs and other areas of Walt Disney World Resort.

5 EPCOT

Walt Disney World Resort
200 EPCOT Center Drive
Orlando, FL 32821; 407-939-5277
disneyworld.disney.go.com/destinations/epcot

EPCOT is one of the four theme parks at Walt Disney World Resort. It celebrates human achievement in technology and features international-culture zones. It is divided into two main areas: Future World and World Showcase. Future World has several pavilions that contain exhibits and rides featuring innovative technology. These include Spaceship Earth, Innoventions, Mission: Space, Test Track, The Seas with Nemo & Friends, The Land, Imagination!, and a seasonal festival center. The World Showcase resembles a permanent World's Fair with 11 themed pavilions, each representing a specific country: Canada, China, France, Germany, Italy, Japan, Mexico, Morocco, Norway, the United Kingdom, and the USA. Each pavilion has themed architecture along with shops and restaurants typical of the country's culture and cuisine.

THE JAPAN PAVILION, PART OF THE WORLD SHOWCASE AREA OF EPCOT, ORLANDO

6 FUN SPOT AMERICA

5700 Fun Spot Way
Orlando, FL 32819; 407-363-3867
fun-spot.com

Fun Spot America is located on the busy International Drive entertainment corridor in Orlando. It has four go-kart tracks and two roller coasters, including Florida's only wooden coaster. The park also has five thrill rides, including the world's second-tallest SkyCoaster at 250 feet. In this ride, one to three riders are winched to the top of a tall launch arch and then suddenly dropped. They swing back and forth on a tether until finally coming to rest, somewhat like in bungee jumping.

7 ICON PARK

8401 International Drive, #100
Orlando, FL 32819; 407-601-7907
iconparkorlando.com

The Orlando Eye is a 400-foot-tall observation wheel that can be seen for miles and is illuminated at night by colored lights. The wheel is part of a complex of shops, restaurants, and other attractions on International Drive. The owners call it an observation wheel rather than a Ferris wheel because the capsule in which you ride is stabilized and doesn't swing back and forth. The wheel has 30 air-conditioned passenger capsules, each with a capacity of 15 people. The view from each carriage is spectacular, and the ride takes about 22 minutes. You can see area hotels, SeaWorld, Universal Orlando, and downtown Orlando. At the top, you can see Walt Disney World, including Space Mountain, Spaceship Earth, and Disney's Contemporary Resort. On clear days, you might even see the Atlantic Ocean, more than 50 miles east.

8 LEGOLAND FLORIDA RESORT

1 LEGOLAND Way
Winter Haven, FL 33884
888-690-5346
legoland.com/florida

The 150-acre LEGOLAND Florida Resort is built on the former Cypress Gardens theme park and preserves many reminders of that property's history, such as a banyan tree that was planted as a seedling in 1939. LEGOLAND has more than 50 rides and attractions, along with shows, shops, restaurants, and a water park, all based on LEGO brands and characters. The resort also has three hotels: the LEGOLAND Hotel has 152 rooms. The LEGOLAND Beach Retreat has 166 rooms in 83 freestanding bungalows designed to look like giant LEGO sets. The LEGOLAND Pirate Island Hotel has 150 rooms furnished in a pirate design. Daily events at the park feature a water-ski show that includes humans and costumed LEGO characters like Captain Brickbeard. Fun things for the kids to do include building a LEGO car and testing it on a digitally timed track.

9 SEAWORLD ORLANDO

7007 Sea World Drive
Orlando, FL 32821; 407-545-5550
seaworld.com/orlando

At SeaWorld Orlando, dolphins, manta rays, sea lions, and other marine creatures are featured throughout, and many perform in shows. You can get close to many of the animals and interact with them. The park features three roller coasters: Kraken (a floorless coaster), Manta (a coaster designed to mimic the movement of a manta ray), and Mako (named for one of the fastest sharks). It is also home to the original Journey to Atlantis water ride. Various nighttime shows feature fireworks; music; and performances by sea lions, otters, or dolphins.

DOLPHIN AT SEAWORLD, ORLANDO

JURASSIC RIVER AT UNIVERSAL ORLANDO RESORT, ORLANDO

10 SPOOK HILL

Fifth Street
adjacent to Spook Hill Elementary School on Dr. J. A. Wiltshire Avenue
Lake Wales, FL 33853
florida-backroads-travel.com/spook-hill.html

Spook Hill is a free optical-illusion attraction that has been entertaining people for a long time. The illusion happens when you park your car at the bottom of the hill and put the car in neutral. The car appears to be coasting slowly up the hill, defying gravity. A white line has been painted on the street so you know where to park your car. If all goes as expected, your car will start its self-powered trip up the hill. Although there are several folk legends—involving ghostly pirates and alligators—about why this happens, the truth is that the lay of the land and growth pattern of the trees make it look like up is down and vice versa. It doesn't matter to you because you will still experience that mystical feeling of beating gravity at its own game.

11 UNIVERSAL ORLANDO RESORT

6000 Universal Boulevard
Orlando, FL 32819; 407-363-8000
universalorlando.com

Universal Orlando is the second-largest resort in Orlando, surpassed in acreage only by Walt Disney World. It consists of two theme parks: Universal Studios Florida and Universal Islands of Adventure. It also includes a water park called Volcano Bay, a nighttime entertainment complex called Universal CityWalk, and six hotels. Each theme park is unique. Universal Studios Florida is made up of themed areas and attractions based on pop-culture icons, TV shows, and movies. The eight themed areas are designed to make you feel like you are on a movie set. Universal Islands of Adventure consists of seven distinct simulated islands, each themed to various adventures. The Wizarding World of Harry Potter is one of the most popular attractions here. Universal CityWalk is located at the entrance, and visitors travel on moving, covered walkways to either of the two main theme parks.

12 WALT DISNEY WORLD RESORT

Walt Disney World Resort
Orlando, FL 32830; 407-939-5277
disneyworld.disney.go.com

Walt Disney World Resort is the most visited vacation resort in the world, covering more than 25,000 acres and featuring six theme parks (Magic Kingdom; EPCOT; Disney's Hollywood Studios; Animal Kingdom; Toy Story Land; and the newest attraction, Star Wars: Galaxy's Edge); two water parks (Typhoon Lagoon and Blizzard Beach); more than 25 themed resort hotels; four golf courses; an RV park; and many entertainment and shopping venues, including Disney Springs. The resort has an annual attendance of more than 52 million. There are so many things to see and do that one could easily spend a month and not see it all. There are always special events underway, and Disney offers ticket packages to include one or more theme parks for 1–10 days. Their website is an indispensable resource to see what's currently available.

13 WEEKI WACHEE SPRINGS STATE PARK

6131 Commercial Way
Spring Hill, FL 34606; 352-592-5656
weekiwachee.com

The Weeki Wachee Springs mermaid show was one of Florida's earliest pre-Disney attractions and is now part of the Florida state park system. Mermaid shows are still being held daily, and Buccaneer Bay, a water park with four waterslides, has been open for nearly 40 years. Don't be surprised if you see other Floridian natives swimming with the mermaids. These include turtles, fish, manatees, otters, and even an occasional gator. You can also rent inner tubes or kayaks and drift down the river.

THE CINDERELLA CASTLE ALL LIT UP, ORLANDO

ART DECO TROPICAL PATTERN, MIAMI BEACH

The arts in Florida include a wide variety of forms that reflect the state's diverse culture.

In addition to hundreds of private art galleries, Florida has a large variety of museums that feature styles ranging from fine art to sidewalk art. From street musicians and symphony orchestras to Broadway musicals in modern performing arts centers, you will find it here. Folk music is part of the cultural fabric, and the state is home to the annual Florida Folk Festival. Dozens of community theaters add to the entertainment opportunities across the state.

Welcome to THE ARTS

An eclectic group of African Americans known as the Florida Highwaymen created a unique art style. Their landscape paintings are prized by collectors and displayed in many museums.

THE RINGLING MUSEUM OF ART, SARASOTA

Find out more about
THE ARTS

14 APPLETON MUSEUM OF ART

College of Central Florida
1333 East Silver Springs Boulevard
Ocala, FL 34470; 352-291-4455
appletonmuseum.org

The Appleton is a stunning example of classically inspired architecture built of Italian travertine marble. Of the museum's 81,610 square feet, 30,000 are devoted to gallery space for the permanent collections, which include works from America, Asia, Africa, and Iran. The museum also houses a 250-seat auditorium, an art library, three spaces for use as art studios or classrooms, and a courtyard café.

15 ARTIS—NAPLES

5833 Pelican Bay Boulevard
Naples, FL 34108; 239-597-1900
artisnaples.org

The 8.5-acre Artis—Naples complex includes The Baker Museum and the performing home of the Naples Philharmonic. The orchestra performs a full schedule each season; additional entertainment offerings include Broadway musicals and dance performances. The museum's permanent collection includes the works of American, European, and Mexican artists. Special exhibitions include some of the most famous artists in the world.

16 ASOLO REPERTORY THEATRE

5555 North Tamiami Trail
Sarasota, FL 34243; 941-351-8000
asolorep.org

Asolo Repertory Theatre is one of the most recognized cultural organizations in Florida. It stages up to 15 productions every season, ranging from new plays to reinterpretations of classical and contemporary works. This theater is an important part of Sarasota's arts scene and has a large resident staff of more than 100, including artists and technical craftspeople. Its resident acting company is complemented by award-winning directors, designers, and guest artists who come from all over the world.

17 BROWARD CENTER FOR THE PERFORMING ARTS

201 SW Fifth Avenue
Fort Lauderdale, FL 33312
954-462-0222
browardcenter.org

The Broward is in a parklike setting overlooking the New River in downtown Fort Lauderdale. It is ranked in the top-10 most-visited theaters in the world. More than 700,000 patrons enjoy the center's more than 700 performances each year. Among these are Broadway musicals, ballets, operas, concerts, plays, lectures, and workshops. Additional educational events serve more than 150,000 students each year.

18 CUMMER MUSEUM

829 Riverside Avenue
Jacksonville, FL 32204; 904-356-6857
cummermuseum.org

The Cummer has one of the finest permanent art collections in Florida, with nearly 5,000 objects dating from 2100 B.C. through modern times and several special collections, such as the Wark Collection of Early Meissen Porcelain. The museum's 2.5-acre garden is a historic example of early 20th-century design. Reflecting pools, fountains, arbors, and sculptures complement the majestic Cummer Oak, whose canopy spans more than 150 feet. This oak is one of the oldest trees in Jacksonville.

19 THE DALÍ MUSEUM

1 Dali Boulevard
St. Petersburg, FL 33701; 727-823-3767
thedali.org

The Dalí is first and foremost an "artist's museum" built to showcase the art, archives, and life history of a single artist, in this case, Salvador Dalí. Although Dalí is most famous for his works of surrealist art, visitors come away from this museum with a new appreciation of how talented in all genres of art he truly was. The permanent collection includes sculpture, prints, photographs, works on paper, paintings, and more. The breadth of his talent was amazing.

20 DR. PHILLIPS CENTER FOR THE PERFORMING ARTS

445 South Magnolia Avenue
Orlando, FL 32801; 407-839-0119
drphillipscenter.org

Dr. Phillips Center is a hub for international, national, and local artists in downtown Orlando, as well as a community outreach center. The two-block area includes the Walt Disney Theater, the Alexis & Jim Pugh Theater, the DeVos Family Room, the Seneff Arts Plaza, and many other spaces set aside for private events. A school of the arts is also in the complex. With performances ranging from Broadway musicals to ballets and comedy acts to children's shows, this center has become a tourist destination that locals also love.

21 FLORIDA THEATRE

128 East Forsyth Street
Jacksonville, FL 32202; 904-355-5661
floridatheatre.com

The Florida Theatre is a historic movie theater in downtown Jacksonville. First opened in 1927, it is on the National Register of Historic Places. After numerous renovations, it is now a local and regional center for the performing arts. In addition to offering 200 cultural and entertainment events each year, including ballet, opera, pop, jazz, rock, country, blues, plays, and movies, the theater also serves as a venue for school graduations and charity events that support local churches, hospitals, and civic groups.

22 KRAVIS CENTER FOR THE PERFORMING ARTS

701 Okeechobee Boulevard
West Palm Beach, FL 33401
561-833-8300
kravis.org

Located in downtown West Palm Beach, the Kravis Center offers an extensive schedule of events that includes Broadway musicals, famous entertainers, and numerous educational events for the community.

The center comprises a concert hall, two black-box theaters, and an events facility. In 2016, the Kravis Center became the first performing arts center in the world to install and feature a custom-designed digital organ in its productions.

23 LAKE PLACID MURALS

Lake Placid Chamber/Mural Gallery
18 North Oak Street,
Lake Placid, FL 33852; 863-465-4335
tourlakeplacid.com

Downtown Lake Placid has one of the largest outdoor art displays in Florida. These displays are in the form of murals on building walls, and they celebrate the history of the area. At last count, there were 47 historic murals. In addition to the murals, the local mural society has added nearly 100 pieces of artwork throughout the town. In 2013, Lake Placid won the award of "America's Most Interesting Town" after a nationwide search by *Reader's Digest*.

24 THE MENNELLO MUSEUM OF AMERICAN ART

900 East Princeton Street
Orlando, FL 32803; 407-246-4278
mennellomuseum.org

The Mennello Museum, located in Loch Haven Cultural Park, offers visitors green space, lake views, and walking trails. The museum's mission is to preserve, display, and interpret the permanent collection of paintings by Earl Cunningham, a 20th-century American folk artist who painted mostly landscapes of the Atlantic Coast. It also features ever-changing exhibits from other outstanding traditional and contemporary American artists across a broad range of disciplines.

25 THE RINGLING MUSEUM OF ART

5401 Bayshore Road
Sarasota, FL 34243; 941-359-5700
ringling.org/museum-art

The John and Mable Ringling Museum of Art is the official art museum for the state of Florida. The huge museum contains 21 galleries of European paintings as well as many pieces of Asian, American, and contemporary art. All told, there are more than 28,000 objects in the museum. The Ringling complex includes the art museum; a circus museum; the Asolo Repertory Theater; and Ca' d'Zan, the mansion of John and Mable Ringling.

26 WYNWOOD WALLS

Wynwood Art District
Miami, FL; 305-531-4411
thewynwoodwalls.com

Wynwood Walls is one of the world's largest outdoor street-art museums, located close to downtown Miami. The walls of the buildings in Wynwood are decorated by constantly changing murals by some of the world's most gifted and famous graffiti and street artists. You can either walk the neighborhood on your own or sign up for a private walking tour led by local artists.

FAMILY WALKING ON A BEAUTIFUL WHITE SAND BEACH ON SUMMER VACATION IN FLORIDA

No matter what kind of beach you are looking for, Florida probably has it.

Florida has the second-longest saltwater shoreline in the United States, behind only Alaska, and the Environmental Protection Agency says the state has 576 beaches, with a total beach length of 825 miles. From sunbathing to long walks, relaxing with a good book or good friends, treasure hunting, or searching for unique birds or seashells, you can find it here.

Welcome to

BEACHES & SEASHELLS

Find out more about BEACHES & SEASHELLS

27 ANNA MARIA ISLAND

Anna Maria Island Chamber of Commerce
5313 Gulf Drive
Holmes Beach, FL 34217; 941-778-1541
annamariaislandchamber.org

The beaches on the Gulf Coast have powdery white sand and are soft beneath your feet, and Anna Maria Island's are no exception. The sand is composed of very fine quartz crystals, and this keeps it from getting too hot to lie or step on, making it great for sunbathing and walking. The surf is rarely too rough; it's just wavy enough for a boogie board or to enjoy splashing around in the shallow water. Another plus is that, unlike many other beaches in Florida, Anna Maria Island's are not lined with high-rise condos.

28 BAILEY-MATTHEWS NATIONAL SHELL MUSEUM & AQUARIUM

3075 Sanibel Captiva Road
Sanibel, FL 33957; 239-395-2233
shellmuseum.org

My grandmother loved to collect shells. She died too soon to experience this museum, which opened to the public in 1995. The museum operates as a reference center for scientists and amateur collectors. Shells from all over the world are on display; many of them are from the Sanibel and Captiva Islands. The museum also has a memorial garden dedicated to actor Raymond Burr, who owned an island in Fiji and helped raise funds to build the museum. Scientists lead daily hour-long beach walks to teach you about local shells.

29 CALADESI ISLAND

Offshore Island
Dunedin, FL 34698; 727-469-5918
floridastateparks.org/parks-and-trails/caladesi-island-state-park

Caladesi is one of the few remaining untouched islands on the Florida Gulf Coast. It is accessible by private boat, the Caladesi Island Ferry, or by walking from Clearwater Beach. The ferry dock is on Honeymoon Island, connected by causeway to the town of Dunedin. The island's 3 miles of unspoiled, pristine white-sand beaches make it perfect for swimming, sunbathing, shelling, boating, fishing, and snorkeling. You can also enjoy kayaking through a 3-mile mangrove trail or camping on your boat at the marina.

A SANIBEL ISLAND SEASHELL COLLECTION, SANIBEL

30 FORT DE SOTO PARK

3500 Pinellas Bayway South
Tierra Verde, FL 33715; 727-582-2100
pinellascounty.org/park/05_ft_desoto.htm

Fort De Soto Park is the largest park in the Pinellas County park system, with 1,136 acres. Visitors reach it from the mainland via FL 679. The five interconnected islands that make up the park are among the best-preserved ecosystems in Florida and feature 3 miles of some of the most beautiful white-sand beaches in the United States. Things to do include visiting the historic fort, camping, swimming, hiking, kayaking, biking, and fishing from a park pier.

31 LITTLE TALBOT ISLAND STATE PARK

12157 Heckscher Drive
Jacksonville, FL 32226; 904-251-2320
floridastateparks.org/parks-and-trails/little-talbot-island-state-park

This park is about 25 miles northeast of Jacksonville on one of the few remaining barrier islands on Florida's east coast. You will enjoy nature at its finest, with maritime forests, desertlike dunes, and pristine salt marshes. The streams on the west side of the park, in addition to the Atlantic surf, provide great opportunities for beachcombing and fishing. Catches include trout, redfish, flounder, and black drum. There is also a campground in the park.

32 SANIBEL AND CAPTIVA ISLANDS

1159 Causeway Road
Sanibel Island, FL 33957; 239-472-1080
sanibel-captiva.org

My grandmother lived in Venice but loved to travel to Sanibel Island for the magnificent shells she would find on the beach. She spent many joyous hours in the "Sanibel stoop," the bent-over posture assumed by shell seekers. There are other things to do on Sanibel, of course, including biking, fishing, bird-watching, boating, golfing, and snorkeling. But shelling remains a popular activity for thousands of visitors. In 2017, *Travel & Leisure* magazine ranked Sanibel Island the best shelling beach in North America.

33 TIGERTAIL BEACH PARK

430 Hernando Drive
Marco Island, FL 34145; 239-252-4000
collierparks.com/collier_park/tigertail-beach-park/

Marco Island is highly developed, but Tigertail Beach is a tranquil, wild place in the middle of it all. The developed part of the beach park has a parking lot, changing rooms, and a snack bar. The park faces a shallow saltwater lagoon. You can either use this beach or wade across the lagoon to another one. Sometimes the water is waist-deep or more, but once you have crossed over, you will find a 3-mile-long beach made of soft, white sand. Most of the beach is wild, and all of it is undeveloped.

34 TOPSAIL HILL PRESERVE STATE PARK

7525 West FL 30A
Santa Rosa Beach, FL 32459
850-267-8330
floridastateparks.org/park/topsail-hill

When you are offshore on a boat in the Gulf, the tall white-sand dunes in this park resemble the sails of sailing ships. The tallest of the majestic dunes, which stretch for 3 miles and are made of sediments rich in white quartz, rises 25 feet above sea level. The beaches are among the best in Florida for swimming, fishing, sunbathing, or just beachcombing, and the adjacent park is an oasis for hikers and bird-watchers.

CRYSTAL RIVER MANATEE SWIM, CRYSTAL RIVER

Florida's mild climate makes it home to an amazing variety of animals.

Millions of birds stop by on their annual migratory journeys, and a similar number stay here year-round. The state is surrounded by salt water and is home to multitudes of dolphins, which are friendly and smart mammals. Manatees, also known as sea cows, can't survive in waters below 68°F, so they congregate in various warmer waters around the state in the cold months. There are countless opportunities in Florida to observe and interact with these creatures, especially around Florida's many springs.

Welcome to

BIRDS, DOLPHINS, MANATEES & MORE

Marineland Studios was one of Florida's first major tourist attractions. Today, it operates as a research center for the study of dolphins.

Sarasota

This 10-acre tropical jungle hosts an amazing flock of friendly pink flamingos.

Chipley

Learn about these amazing creatures and become a virtual member of a wolf pack.

GULF FRITILLARY THAT CAN BE FOUND AT BUTTERFLY WORLD, COCONUT CREEK

Find out more about
BIRDS, DOLPHINS, MANATEES & MORE

35 BUTTERFLY WORLD

Tradewinds Park
3600 West Sample Road
Coconut Creek, FL 33073
954-977-4434
butterflyworld.com

Opened in 1988, Butterfly World is located about 45 minutes north of Fort Lauderdale in Tradewinds Park. Home to more than 20,000 live butterflies, it is the largest butterfly park in the world. It also has the country's largest free-flight hummingbird aviary.

36 CRYSTAL RIVER MANATEE SWIM

American Pro Diving Center
821 US 19
Crystal River, FL 34429; 352-563-0041
americanprodiving.com

Crystal River is a small town 70 miles north of Tampa, where West Indian manatees like to congregate in crystal-clear waters where the temperature is 72°F. Manatees cannot survive in water that is colder than 68°F, so this location is perfect for them. American Pro Diving Center offers several snorkel tours that let you visit with these giant, gentle creatures. The best time to visit is November–March, when you can swim with the manatees or just observe them from a boat or a dock in Kings Bay.

37 FARM TOURS OF OCALA

World Equestrian Center
1750 NW 80th Avenue
Ocala, FL 32668; 352-895-9302
farmtoursofocala.com

Here you will enjoy a 3.25-hour guided tour of the working farms in Ocala, one of only four major thoroughbred centers in the world. Considered the Horse Capital of the World (along with Lexington, Kentucky), Marion County produced American Pharoah, Triple Crown Winner of 2015; Nyquist, winner of the 2016 Kentucky Derby; and other winning horses. On the tour, you'll go behind the scenes and chat with the professionals who train and care for these thoroughbreds.

38 THE FLORIDA AQUARIUM

701 Channelside Drive
Tampa, FL 33602; 813-273-4000
flaquarium.org

The kid-friendly Florida Aquarium often appears on lists of the country's best aquariums. The museum has many innovative ways to tell visitors all about the ecological cycles of Florida's unique water systems. Interactive programs such as "SeaTREK" and "Sloth Encounter" let you do things like dive underwater and feed animals. The aquarium also has an outdoor fun zone with a splash pad, sandboxes, and other activities for kids.

39 GULFARIUM MARINE ADVENTURE PARK

1010 Miracle Strip Parkway SE
Fort Walton Beach, FL 32548
850-243-9046
gulfarium.com

Since 1955, Gulfarium Marine Adventure Park has sought to inspire its guests to respect and preserve marine life by providing educational and entertaining experiences for people of all ages. The numerous animal encounters offered include those with dolphins, stingrays, gators, reptiles, turtles, penguins, seals, sea lions, and birds. They even have an experience called Breakfast with the Dolphins. Most of the encounters require a reservation.

40 J. N. "DING" DARLING NATIONAL WILDLIFE REFUGE

1 Wildlife Drive
Sanibel, FL 33957; 239-472-1100
fws.gov/refuge/jn_ding_darling

Located on Sanibel Island, this 6,400-acre refuge is part of the National Wildlife Refuge System. It is named for cartoonist and conservationist Jay Norwood "Ding" Darling. The refuge was established in 1945 to protect one of the country's largest undeveloped mangrove ecosystems and is well-known for its migratory bird populations. You can learn more at the Visitor & Education Center, view birds and wildlife on the Indigo Trail, and explore the Bailey Tract wetland.

41 JUNGLE ISLAND

1111 Parrot Jungle Trail
Miami, FL 33132; 305-400-7000
jungleisland.com

Jungle Island has been around for more than 80 years in one form or another. Once called Parrot Jungle and located south of Miami, it was famous for letting birds fly free—without cages. The attraction moved to its current location on downtown Watson Island in 2003 and changed its name to Jungle Island in 2007. It is home to more than 300 birds and other exotic animals, including rare twin orangutans. The birds still fly free.

42 MARINELAND DOLPHIN ADVENTURE

9600 Ocean Shore Boulevard
St. Augustine, FL 32080
407-563-4701
marineland.net

Marineland was founded in 1938 as Marine Studios and was the filming location of many movies. The name was later changed, and the first-ever dolphin performances were held here. Today there are no shows where dolphins perform before large audiences, but visitors can interact with dolphins by swimming with them or assisting a trainer in working and playing with the animals. There are also tours and exhibits where you can get a close look at other sea life, including eels, rays, octopi, sea turtles, and sharks.

43 MIAMI SEAQUARIUM

4400 Rickenbacker Causeway
Miami, FL 33149; 305-361-5705
miamiseaquarium.com

Miami Seaquarium—filming location for the TV show *Flipper*—is a 38-acre attraction that offers many child-friendly experiences that the entire family will enjoy. You can see and interact with dolphins, sea lions, stingrays, sharks, birds, fish, and even penguins. Watch the animals perform and learn about their lifestyle at shows such as the Flipper Dolphin Show and the Manatee Exhibit. And for a hands-on, behind-the-scenes experience, you can participate in the Trainer for a Day program. The Seaquarium is open 365 days a year.

44 MOTE MARINE LABORATORY & AQUARIUM

1600 Ken Thompson Parkway
Sarasota, FL 34236; 941-388-4441
mote.org

Mote is an independent research institution that originally specialized in the study of sharks but in recent years has greatly increased its scope. Its scientists now study the population dynamics of manatees, dolphins, sea turtles, sharks, and coral reefs. Visitors are welcome to enjoy the working aquarium, which has two touch tanks, a 135,000-gallon shark habitat, and more than 100 species of marine life.

45 RETIREMENT HOME FOR HORSES AT MILL CREEK FARM

20307 NW CR 235A
Alachua, FL 32615; 386-462-1001
millcreekfarm.org

The owners of Mill Creek Farm wanted to do something to help horses too old to be ridden or used in various businesses and police departments. They also wanted to help abused horses that had been rescued by the SPCA or other humane societies. The farm, open to visitors on Saturdays, has more than 335 rolling acres of tree-lined pastureland for the horses to wander around freely. There are about 100 horses living there at any given time. You can meet some of them for an admission fee of two carrots.

46 SARASOTA JUNGLE GARDENS

3701 Bayshore Road
Sarasota, FL 34234; 941-355-5305
sarasotajunglegardens.com

Sarasota Jungle Gardens is a 10-acre tropical site that is home to more than 200 native and exotic animals, including birds of prey, parrots, macaws, primates, small mammals, dozens of snakes, lizards, iguanas, alligators, crocodiles, and other reptiles. A favorite of visitors is the population of Floridian pink flamingos. The flamingos are friendly and often greet guests personally and face-to-face. One may feed them by hand or just enjoy watching them strut by.

47 SEACREST WOLF PRESERVE

3449 Bonnett Pond Road
Chipley, FL 32428; 850-773-2897
seacrestwolfpreserve.org

At this preserve, you can become part of the pack as you walk through large natural habitats that are home to gray, Arctic, and British Columbian wolves. The hands-on experience allows visitors as young as age 10 to interact with and learn about this amazing species. Saturday Wolf Encounter Tours last approximately 3 hours, with a break along the way, as well as places to stop and rest. All tours are by reservation only; call the preserve to schedule one.

OLD BOOKS AT A VINTAGE BOOKSTORE

Stepping into a bookstore offers an opportunity to slow down in a world that demands ever-faster movement.

Small, local bookstores offer a personalized, curated experience that big-box stores can't match, and shopping locally keeps money in the neighborhood. Knowledgeable, local staff provide tailored recommendations and may introduce you to indie gems and rare finds such as used books or collectibles. These cozy shops usually stock books by local authors, and many double as community hubs, hosting events and creating connections.

Welcome to

BOOKSTORES

Find out more about BOOKSTORES

48 ALL BOOKED UP

271 Colony Boulevard
The Villages, FL 32162; 352-350-6669

The store sells books, puzzles, audiobooks, and DVDs and hosts many events, including book signings by local authors. You can sell your used books here or trade ones you bought earlier. Open Monday through Saturday, the store's welcoming staff and organized layout make it a great place to visit and shop.

49 ANNETTE'S BOOK NOOK

7205 Estero Boulevard, Suite 701
Fort Myers Beach, FL 33931
239-671-6299

Annette's Book Nook is an independent bookstore that was reborn in January 2025 after Hurricane Ian's devastation badly damaged Fort Myers Beach. The store, owned by Annette Stillson, offers new and used books, island gifts, and a trade-in program.

50 BACK IN THE DAY BOOKS

355 Main Street
Dunedin, FL 34698; 727-221-0025

Back in the Day Books is owned by Boe Rushing, a former lawyer whose passion for books led him to found this bookstore. Though he also carries the latest new books in his shop, Boe served two terms as President of the Florida Antiquarian Booksellers Association. Located in beautiful downtown Dunedin, the store's unique selections have resulted in a large local following. The store is open daily.

51 BARREL OF BOOKS & GAMES

403 North Donnelly Street
Mount Dora, FL 32757; 352-735-1950
barrelofbooksandgames.com

Barrel of Books and Games blends new and used books with board games, puzzles, and gaming supplies. It is owned by Crissy Stile, former Mayor of Mount Dora, who is not only an expert on books but is extremely knowledgeable about her town. The shop has a busy book signing schedule and comfortable places for local book clubs to meet. There was a book signing here for the first edition of *Florida Day Trips by Theme*.

52 BEACH HOUSE BOOKS

3210 Physicians Way
Sebring, FL 33870; 863-304-1079
beachhousebooksandmore.com

Beach House Books is a neat, little independent bookstore located in a physicians' plaza in historic downtown Sebring. It has a curated selection of new and used books ideal for a relaxing day of browsing. When we last visited, they had a wonderful dog taking a peaceful nap on the floor. It is open Tuesday through Saturday.

53 BLUEWATER BOOKS & CHARTS

3233 SW 2nd Avenue
Fort Lauderdale, FL 33315
954-763-6533
bluewaterweb.com

Here you'll find a huge inventory of nautical books, charts, and navigation tools and experts who can tell you all about them. The store also offers a selection of travel and nature books for landlubbers. It is open Monday through Saturday and is a fun place to visit.

54 BOOKS & BOOKS

54A

265 Aragon Avenue
Coral Gables, FL 33134; 305-442-4408
booksandbooks.com

Books & Books is a literary icon in a historic 1927 Mediterranean building in the heart of Coral Gables. Owned by Mitchell Kaplan, who founded the store in 1982, this 9,000-square-foot building not only has books but also a café and courtyard. The store has a busy schedule of author events and community gatherings. Open daily, its architectural charm and wide book selection make it a favorite place for locals and visitors alike.

54B

11297 South Dixie Highway
Pinecrest, FL 33156; 786-552-3290
booksandbooks.com

Books & Books has another location in Pinecrest. This smaller Books & Books store brings Mitchell Kaplan's Coral Gables bookstore charm to this suburb of Miami. It features unique gifts, along with a wide selection of new books.

54C

9700 Collins Avenue
Bal Harbour, FL 305-864-4241
booksandbooks.com

Books & Books opened a location in the Bal Harbour Shops in 2005. The staff prides itself in paying attention to reader trends and seeking out new books their customers will love.

55 THE BOOK MARK

220 1st Street
Neptune Beach, FL 32266
904-241-9026
bookmarkbeach.com

The Book Mark has been busy in Neptune Beach since it opened in 1990. Owner Rona Brinlee hosts frequent author events and book signings, making it a community hub. It is located near the Atlantic Ocean, and its big windows and bright interior make it a standout for locals and visitors. The store is open daily.

56 BOOKSTORE 1 SARASOTA

117 South Pineapple Avenue
Sarasota, FL 34236; 941-400-7735
sarasotabooks.com

Opened in 2011, this shop is well-known for its selection of new books, local-author events, and knowledgeable staff. It is located downtown and is noted for its thoughtful curation and community engagement. Open daily, it's a great place to visit for readers seeking new titles and a busy literary scene in Sarasota.

57 COPPERFISH BOOKS

212 West Virginia Avenue, Suite 112
Punta Gorda, FL 33950; 941-205-2560
copperfishbooks.com

Copperfish Books is located in downtown Punta Gorda. It is an independent store focused on providing the local community with new books, gifts, and frequent author events, including book signings. The store is open Tuesday through Sunday.

58 DOWNTOWN BOOKS & PURL

67 Commerce Street
Apalachicola, FL 32320; 850-653-1290
downtownbooksandpurl.com

Downtown Books & Purl is a quaint combination of a bookstore and yarn shop in the downtown area of Apalachicola. The bookstore offers a diverse mix of genres and local history titles. It has many offbeat finds among its selections. Open daily, it's a serene, hidden gem in this fishing village on Florida's Forgotten Coast.

59 FAMILY BOOK SHOP

1301 North Woodland Boulevard
Deland, FL 32720; 386-736-6501
familybookshopdeland.com

The store has been owned since 2015 by Kerry and Kaaren Johnson. Known for good stock and fair prices, it's a treasure hunter's dream. When I last visited, I met Ink, the bookstore's black cat. The store is open Monday through Saturday and is located near Deland's historic Stetson University.

60 FERN & FABLE

51 West Granada Boulevard
Ormond Beach, FL 32174
386-232-8671
fernandfablebooks.com

You will first notice the beautiful flower mural on the side of the building near the entrance. The store was founded by Rayna Dunlop, a local lady born and raised in Ormond Beach. The small store has occasional local-author events and is a great stop for book lovers. It is open Tuesday through Saturday.

61 HIDDEN LANTERN BOOKSTORE

84 North Barrett Square
Rosemary Beach, FL 32461
850-460-9567
thehiddenlantern.com

Don't let the size fool you; the store is full of warmth, making it a place worth visiting and discovering a book or two to take home. Hidden Lantern is located in the heart of Rosemary Beach's downtown and is surrounded by coffee shops and restaurants.

62 THE LYNX BOOKS

601 South Main Street
Gainesville, FL 32601; 352-215-1117
thelynxbooks.com

This bookshop stocks a wide variety of books, from literature frequently challenged or banned in Florida to classics, children's books, and everything in between. They also host events, including several book clubs.

63 MACINTOSH BOOKS + PAPER

1620 Periwinkle Way
Sanibel, FL 33957; 239-472-1447
macintoshbooks.com/

Macintosh Books + Paper carries a wide selection of new books, many of them island-themed. It also sells puzzles and games along with fine stationery, greeting cards, and unique gifts. Author events and a cozy setup enhance its appeal. Open daily, it's a Sanibel staple for readers seeking quality and a touch of local flavor.

64 MIDTOWN READER

1123 Thomasville Road
Tallahassee, FL 32303
850-425–2665
midtownreader.com

Midtown Reader is an independent neighborhood bookstore owned by Sally Bradshaw. She is a lifelong Floridian who is a mystery lover and history buff. The store features a wide selection of new books and has author events and book signings. The store is open daily and is popular among students and faculty of Tallahassee's Florida State University and Florida A&M University, as well as denizens of the nearby Florida capital complex.

65 THE MUSE BOOKSHOP

112 South Woodland Boulevard
Deland, FL 32720; 386-734-0278

The Muse Bookshop offers new and used books, vinyl records, and an artistic atmosphere in historic downtown DeLand. The store has been a local favorite since 1985. Its eclectic stock, from Floridiana to classics to obscure finds, paired with the creative energy of its founder-owner Janet Bollum, draws browsers and collectors alike. The store is open Tuesday through Saturday.

66 MY FAVORITE BOOKS

1415 Timberland Road, Suite 313
Tallahassee, FL 32312; 850-668-7498
myfavoritebooks.org

Located in a nice, little shopping center in Tallahassee, the store's friendly staff and affordable prices make it a go-to for budget-conscious readers. You can bring in your own used books to trade in. Open Monday through Saturday, this local favorite has a welcoming feel that is perfect for checking out rare volumes and just doing some leisurely browsing.

67 NO NAME BOOKS & GIFTS

325 Reid Avenue
Port Saint Joe, FL 32456
850-229-9277

No Name Books & Gifts pairs used books with coffee, pastries, and light bites in the small-town setting of Port St. Joe on the Gulf Coast. It also has a selection of new books, including some by local authors. It is open Tuesday through Saturday.

68 PORTKEY BOOKS

123 North Bay Hills Boulevard
Safety Harbor, FL 34695
727-248-0211
shop.portkeybooks.com

This small bookstore began as a pop-up shop but was eventually able to move into a small storefront.

69 STORY & SONG BOOKSTORE

1430 Park Avenu,
Fernandina Beach, FL 32034
904-601-2118
storyandsongarts.org

Owners Donna and Mark Paz Kaufman opened the bookstore in 2018. It is not only a bookstore but also a bistro with live performances featuring singers and songwriters often performing Americana music. The shop has a great selection of books, puzzles, and gifts. It also hosts book discussions and literary luncheons. Open daily, the store is located in Amelia Park Town Center south of downtown Fernandina Beach.

"BOOKS" SIGN NEAR A BOOKSTORE

70 SUNDOG BOOKS

89 Central Square
Seaside, FL 32459; 850-231-5481
sundogbooks.com

Open daily, Sundog Books offers new books and beach reads in upscale Seaside, the prototypical "new urban" community on the Gulf Coast. Its tables and shelves of books and gifts make it a stylish and relaxing place to visit. The shop has a good selection of books by local authors and a lot of information about its part of the state. Be sure to also visit the music shop upstairs.

71 SUNSHINE BOOKSELLERS

677 South Collier Boulevard
Marco Island, FL 34145
239-393-0353

Sunshine Booksellers has two stores on Marco Island: the North (1000 North Collier Boulevard, Suite 14) and the South (677 South Collier Boulevard). Both stores feature new books, unique gifts, and a large selection of toys and puzzles. The North store is also a FedEx Authorized Shipping Center and provides notary services. Open daily, each store makes a great stop for readers looking for good books and gifts.

72 TOMBOLO BOOKS

2153 1st Avenue South
Saint Petersburg, FL 33712
727-755-9456
tombolobooks.com

Tombolo Books in St. Petersburg's Grand Central District has been a local favorite since opening in 2019. The colorful exterior invites you to go inside and browse. Open daily, it has a great selection of new books, author events, and a children's section. The shop also hosts a book club that meets once a month.

73 VERO BEACH BOOK CENTER

392 21st Street
Vero Beach, FL 32960; 772-569-2050
verobeachbookcenter.com

Vero Beach Book Center has been a prominent and popular bookstore since 1975. It moved in recent years into a large, pink two-story building. With books, gifts, and many book signings and other events, it's a local favorite that's open daily.

74 WRITER'S BLOCK BOOKSTORE

74A

312 North Park Avenue, Suite B
Winter Park, FL 32789; 704-385-7084
writersblockbookstore.com

Writer's Block Bookstore on Park Avenue offers new books and author events in one of Florida's most upscale downtown shopping districts. It is popular with the locals and the many visitors who stop by every day. Open daily, it's a stylish stop for readers seeking new books and relaxing browsing.

74B

32 West Plant Street
Winter Garden, FL 34787
407-335-4192
writersblockbookstore.com

Writer's Block Bookstore on historic West Plant Street is the sister store to the location in Winter Park. It is located in a wonderful, historic downtown shopping district. The shop features a good selection of adult and children's books and hosts a lot of events and book signings.

EVERGLADES AIRBOAT RIDE IN SOUTH FLORIDA

Florida has thousands of miles of saltwater coastline, thousands of lakes, and dozens of rivers.

Getting out on the water is a traditional way to enjoy the state and see sights you can't spot from the roads. Tours and adventures are readily available to help you enjoy the water, or you can rent a boat and do it on your own. Snorkeling, fishing, and sailing are activities that Floridians enjoy all year long.

Welcome to
ENJOYING THE WATER

Find out more about ENJOYING THE WATER

75 AJ'S WATER ADVENTURES

116 Harbor Boulevard
Destin, FL 32541; 850-837-2222
dolphincruisesdestinfl.com

AJ's Water Adventures covers almost everything you could want to do on the water. They give you plenty of ways to enjoy the beautiful, clear, emerald waters surrounding this Gulf Coast town. You can go on a dolphin cruise; a sunset cruise; or a leisurely sail on a 74-foot, custom-built schooner named *Daniel Webster Clements*. You can also take a thrilling, high-speed ride on the *Sea Quest*, a 53-foot speedboat. If you want to get into the water, they will take you on a local snorkeling trip. There are several cruise and tour packages to choose from, and every cruise comes with complimentary beer and wine (but not too much), soda, and water. They even let the kids take the helm and be captain every now and then.

76 BOGGY CREEK AIRBOAT ADVENTURES

2001 E. Southport Road
Kissimmee, FL 34746; 407-344-9550
bcairboats.com

No visit to Florida is complete without taking an airboat ride. Moved along by engine-driven aircraft propellers, these shallow-draft craft can go places that ordinary boats can't. Experienced captains operate Boggy Creek's fleet of 12 U.S. Coast Guard–inspected boats, which can carry up to 17 passengers each. Tours come in a variety of options, from half-hour trips to private, 1-hour excursions for families or groups. There's even a tour that lets you drive the airboat. The sunset and night tours are especially interesting. All of the tours will bring you up close to Floridian wildlife, including water birds and alligators. Other attractions here include an Indigenous village, a simulated gemstone-and-fossil mine, and a tiki bar. There is also a barbecue restaurant on-site.

77 CATBOAT ADVENTURES

148 Charles Avenue
Mount Dora, FL 32757; 352-325-1442
catboattour.com

Mount Dora is a charming town on Lake Dora in the hill-and-lake country northwest of Orlando. One of the best ways to enjoy and explore the waters is by small boat. CatBoat Adventures provides you with a Craig Cat, a small twin-hulled boat that is powered by an outboard motor and seats two people side by side. The tour guides have their own boat and take their small fleet of visitors on a narrated tour of Lake Dora and the fascinating, mile-long Dora Canal. This canal is one of the most beautiful in Florida, and boating here is like cruising down a jungle stream among 2,000-year-old cypress trees. You may see herons, egrets, ducks, ospreys, eagles, turtles, and alligators. The canal was used in 1951 to reshoot some of the river scenes from the movie

African Queen, starring Humphrey Bogart and Katharine Hepburn. The tour starts at Mount Dora Boating Center and Marina two blocks from downtown Mount Dora.

78 FLORIDA BAY OUTFITTERS

104050 Overseas Highway
Key Largo, FL 33037; 305-451-3018
floridabayoutfitters.com

This operation is one of Florida's largest retailers and renters of anything related to paddle sports. Their location in the upper Keys is a great place to begin any kind of paddling trip in the Florida Keys and south Florida. You can buy or rent a variety of kayaks, paddleboards, and canoes, and the shop offers hourly or daily tours, as well as longer trips. Take a full-day tour in Everglades National Park; 7 Mile Bridge; Indian Key; or an even longer, two-to-five-day tour of the lower Keys backcountry focusing on wildlife. You can also enjoy a full-moon tour, a paddleboard tour, a snorkel tour, and more, all led by experts. The tours are great for all levels of experience. If you want to supplement your paddling, there's even a full-day adventure on Hobie Beach, sailing kayaks among the islands of Florida Bay.

79 *JUNGLE QUEEN* CRUISES

Bahia Mar Yachting Center
801 Seabreeze Boulevard
Fort Lauderdale, FL 33316
954-462-5596
junglequeen.com

This riverboat cruise will delight you as you glide along the many miles of waterways in Fort Lauderdale. You will learn all about the history of this great town and see the homes of many rich and famous people. The boat holds more than 500 passengers and resembles an Old Florida paddlewheel steamer from the pioneer days of Florida. The cruises take between 90 minutes and 3 hours, and some feature a buffet dinner.

80 KEY WEST EXPRESS

80A

1200 Main Street
Fort Myers Beach, FL 33931
239-463-5733

80B

100 Grinnell Street
Key West, FL 33040; 239-463-5733

80C

951 Bald Eagle Drive
Marco Island, FL 34145; 239-463-5733
keywestexpress.net

The Key West Express is a passenger ferry service with three vessels that operate between Fort Myers Beach, Marco Island, and Key West. It is quite often faster to visit Key West this way than to drive. The fleet consists of the 155-foot *Big Cat Express*, the 140-foot *AtlantiCat*, and the 170-foot *Key West Express*. Each of these twin-hulled craft has a cruising speed of more than 30 knots (about 40 miles per hour). That's faster than the destroyer I served on in the Navy. Both vessels have air-conditioned interiors, several sun decks, a full-service galley and bar, satellite television, and plenty of places to sit and relax. Each boat is fully certified by the U.S. Coast Guard. Travel times between Key West and the other ports (and vice versa) are usually about 3.5 hours, depending on the weather. Boarding time from Fort Myers Beach and Marco Island is usually 7 a.m. From Key West, boarding begins at either 4 or 5 p.m. You can also depart and return on different days.

81 *NAPLES PRINCESS* CRUISES

550 Port O Call Way
Naples, FL 34102; 239-649-2275
naplesprincesscruises.com

The *Naples Princess* is a 105-foot luxury yacht approved by the Coast Guard for up to 149 passengers. It is often used for private charters and parties but also offers daily public cruises. The yacht has a beautiful cherry-wood interior and gold-plated, reflective ceilings. It's a wonderful place to view the historical landmarks and luxury mansions of Naples and some wildlife as well. The daily public cruises begin from the docks at Port of Naples Marina across from Tin City, near downtown Naples. The yacht cruises leisurely down Naples Bay to view the magnificent homes in Port Royal, then out Gordon Pass to the Gulf. If you are on the sunset tour, this is where you will watch one of the famous Gulf sunsets. You are likely to see dolphins and seabirds on your trip. The yacht is equipped with two full-service cash bars.

82 RIVER SAFARIS

10823 West Yulee Drive
Homosassa, FL 34448; 352-628-5222
riversafaris.com

River Safaris is in Old Homosassa on a waterway that leads to the Homosassa River and passes Monkey Island. You can spend a day in Homosassa, basing your adventures from there. They have airboat tours, boat rentals, pontoon boat tours, manatee tours, scalloping and fishing adventures, a gift shop with local art, three alligators who live in a pen on-site, and more. Try the 2-hour twilight, dolphin-watching, and tiki bar pontoon tour.

83 SCENIC BOAT TOUR

312 East Morse Boulevard
Winter Park, FL 32789; 407-644-4056
scenicboattours.com

The Winter Park Scenic Boat Tour has been entertaining visitors since 1938. It is only an hour-long ride, but you will have plenty of fun during that hour. The pontoon boats cruise on a route between Lakes Osceola, Virginia, and Maitland, passing some of the most expensive real estate in Florida. You will see many tropical trees and plants along the route, especially in the canals that connect the lakes. You will also learn about the famous structures in Winter Park and who lived there then and who lives there now. The tour guides are local captains who know the lake area well and keep you interested from beginning to end.

84 THE SCHOONER *FREEDOM*

111 Avenida Menendez
St. Augustine, FL 32084
904-810-1010
schoonerfreedom.com

I love to sail, and this is an easy way to do it. Enjoy seeing the sights of St. Augustine and learning about its fascinating history aboard the schooner *Freedom*, a 76-foot, gaff-rigged topsail vessel that is well-known around these waters. Captain John Zaruba and his wife, Admiral Sarah, have been sailing the schooner in St. Augustine since 2001. You can pitch in and help sail the boat or just relax and enjoy a complimentary drink. If the weather is OK, John and Sarah might even let you take the helm. There is plenty of protected water around St. Augustine, and the schooner goes wherever the wind takes it. You will typically see some dolphins on the trip, as well as seabirds and other wildlife. Day sails, sunset sails, and moonlight sails are offered. The day sails take about 2 hours.

85 ST. JOHNS RIVERSHIP CO.

433 North Palmetto Avenue
Sanford, FL 32771; 321-441-3030
stjohnsrivershipco.com

Any journey on the north-flowing St. Johns River is a trip into Florida history. This river has been a major transportation route for centuries, and many of the state's oldest towns are along its shores, yet it still has miles of pristine, undeveloped shoreline. The St. Johns Rivership Co. offers a comfortable way to enjoy the river on the *Barbara-Lee*, a 105-foot, modern ship built to resemble the stern-wheelers of old. The five-deck vessel features ornate wrought-iron railings and massive wooden paddle wheels and can handle 176 passengers. *Barbara-Lee* departs from downtown Sanford almost every day. Several types of cruises are offered, and all narrated cruises provide you with a well-stocked bar and an entrée prepared by a professional chef. You will cruise along the river, enjoying the view of wildlife and lush vegetation in air-conditioned comfort while enjoying live musical entertainment.

86 WATER TAXI

10 boarding locations
in Fort Lauderdale
954-467-6677
watertaxi.com

The water taxi is an enjoyable way to visit and explore the Fort Lauderdale area. You can enjoy your trip as an individual, a family, or a group (by reservation). As you cruise along the waterways, your captain will point out mansions of famous people and landmarks and fill you in on the history of the area you are visiting. You will see hundreds of mega yachts, as Fort Lauderdale is the yachting capital of the world. Buy an all-day pass to board a vessel at any of 10 locations and ride the taxi all day (find a map of the locations on the website). You can also buy happy-hour passes and monthly passes. It is good manners to leave your crew members a tip.

WATER TAXI CROSSING ON THE INTRACOASTAL WATERWAY, FORT LAUDERDALE

THIS ANHINGA HAS JUST CAUGHT AN ARMORED CATFISH, EVERGLADES NATIONAL PARK, SHARK VALLEY, MIAMI

The Florida Everglades spans over a million acres and is one of the important and impressive natural areas in North America.

It is a huge, subtropical wetland of sawgrass marshes set within a complex of interdependent ecosystems. These ecosystems include cypress swamps, the estuarine mangrove forests of the Ten Thousand Islands, tropical hardwood hillocks, pine rocklands, and the saltwater marine environment of Florida Bay in the Keys.

Welcome to

THE EVERGLADES

Find out more about THE EVERGLADES

87 BIG CYPRESS NATIONAL PRESERVE

87A
Big Cypress Swamp Welcome Center
33000 Tamiami Trail East
Ochopee, FL 34141; 239-695-4757

87B
Oasis Visitor Center
52105 Tamiami Trail East
Ochopee, FL 34141; 239-695-4111
nps.gov/bicy

This 729,000-acre preserve was established in 1974. Unlike at adjacent Everglades National Park, the Seminole and Miccosukee Indians were given permanent rights to occupy and use portions of the land. Some live here and provide guided tours. There are two visitor centers on Tamiami Trail where you can learn about the history of the preserve and watch an informational film in which park-service staffers tell you what activities are available. The preserve is home to mangroves, orchids, alligators, snakes, birds, otters, bobcats, coyotes, black bears, and panthers. Hiking is a popular activity all year long because the trails are more walkable than those in the sawgrass prairies of the Everglades farther east. You can also arrange canoe or kayak trips, and tent, RV, and backcountry campsites are available. The preserve is designated a Dark Sky Place by DarkSky International. Far away from the urban development of the East and West Coasts, the preserve has a night sky where you can still see thousands of stars and enjoy the Milky Way.

88 CLYDE BUTCHER'S BIG CYPRESS GALLERY

52388 Tamiami Trail
Ochopee, FL 34141; 239-695-2428
clydebutcher.com/galleries

Photographer Clyde Butcher specializes in large-format, black-and-white landscape photographs, especially of the Everglades. He has been called "the next Ansel Adams." A large collection of his photographs are on view in his Big Cypress Gallery, which is about 0.5 mile east of the Big Cypress National Preserve Oasis Visitor Center. The artist has other galleries in Venice and Sarasota as well. A popular feature of this gallery is the Big Cypress Swamp Walk, conducted by Clyde himself. On this 2-hour eco-swamp tour, you will get your feet wet and see orchids, ferns, bromeliads, birds, and many other swamp creatures. If you like, you can book a few nights at the Everglades Swamp Cottage or Niki's Bungalow, located behind the gallery. These lodgings have all the modern conveniences and tremendous views of the natural surroundings.

89 EVERGLADES NATIONAL PARK

89A
Gulf Coast Visitor Center
815 Oyster Bar Lane
Everglades City, FL 34139
239-695-3311

89B
Shark Valley Visitor Center
36000 SW Eighth Street

(US 41/Tamiami Trail)
Miami, FL 33194; 305-221-8776

89C

Ernest F. Coe Visitor Center
40001 FL 9336
Homestead, FL 33034; 305-242-7700

89D

Flamingo Visitor Center
1 Flamingo Lodge Highway
Homestead, FL 33034; 239-695-2945
nps.gov/ever

This national park's 1.5 million acres make it the largest tropical wilderness in the United States. It is a sensitive ecosystem of wetlands and forests in what Marjory Stoneman Douglas called the "River of Grass." This shallow, slow-moving river flows south from Lake Okeechobee toward Florida Bay. Thirty-six threatened or endangered species can be found in the park, including the Florida panther, the West Indian manatee, 10 species of birds, 8 species of plants, 7 species of invertebrates, and 8 species of reptiles. The best time to visit is from December to March, when temperatures are cooler and mosquitoes are least active. There are four entrances at separate visitor centers. The two closest entrances to Miami are the Ernest Coe Visitor Center and the Shark Valley Visitor Center. At the Ernest Coe Visitor Center in Homestead, a 38-mile road begins, meandering through rockland, cypress, freshwater, and coastal prairies, as well as mangrove forests, and ending at the Flamingo Visitor Center and marina, which is open only during the busiest time of the year. I prefer the Gulf Coast entrance in Everglades City, which is closest to Naples and the western coast. This entrance provides boat tours and exhibits. It is also where canoes can access the Everglades Wilderness Waterway, a 99-mile canoe trail that extends to the Flamingo Visitor Center. The western coast of the park and the Ten Thousand Islands are accessible only by boat.

90 LAKE OKEECHOBEE SCENIC TRAIL

Numerous access points around the perimeter of Lake Okeechobee
863-983-8101
saj.usace.army.mil/LOST

Lake Okeechobee is the largest lake in Florida and is encircled by an earthen dike that is 35 feet high and 110 miles long. The dike was built in the 1930s as a flood-control measure. Although the dike prevents a direct view of the lake from most of the roads around its shores, there is a path on its top that has been made part of the Florida National Scenic Trail. There are unobstructed views of the lake from the top of the dike. About half of the trail's length is paved, and the other half is compacted gravel. The trail can be used for hiking, biking, roller blading, and horseback riding. There are 14 places along the trail that can be used for camping. There are numerous access points along the trail. Since portions of the dike are being reconstructed, the Army Corps of Engineers website continually updates which parts of the trail are available at any given time.

91 MICCOSUKEE INDIAN VILLAGE

Mile marker 36, US 41 (Tamiami Trail)
Miami, FL 33194; 305-552-8365
miccosukee.com/resort/experiences

Most people have heard of the Seminoles, but who are the Miccosukee? They are a separate tribe with some cultural differences, and they broke off from the Seminoles in 1962. In addition to a casino and gaming resort in Miami, the Miccosukee have a village farther west on the Tamiami Trail in the Everglades, about 40 miles west of Miami. Your visit will include a guided tour of the history, culture, and lifestyle of the tribe. You will see demonstrations of wood carving, beadwork, basket weaving, and doll making and learn about alligators and how the tribe has coexisted with them all these years. You can take an airboat ride into the Everglades and visit a traditional camp that has been owned by the same Miccosukee family for more than 100 years. A museum has photos of generations of tribe members, as well as colorful native clothing, native paintings, and other tribal artifacts. The Miccosukee Restaurant serves the famous Miccosukee fry bread and pumpkin bread, plus gator, catfish, frog legs, and more.

92 MUSEUM OF THE EVERGLADES

105 Broadway Avenue West
Everglades City, FL 34139
239-252-5026
colliermuseums.com/locations/museum-of-the-everglades

When you visit this museum, you will enter what used to be a laundry building from the 1920s that served the Rod and Gun Club. Laundry operations ceased many years ago, and the structure is now on the National Register of Historic Places. Inside, the museum documents the history of Everglades City and the surrounding area, which was settled in the late 1800s. Early settlers survived by fishing, farming, and hunting, most making their living from the Everglades in one form or another. A recent exhibit titled *Abandoned Vehicles of the Everglades* highlighted a collection of photographs by Matt Stock that show rusty, long-abandoned vehicles that have become part of the ecosystem as the Floridian jungle grows up, into, and through them.

93 ROD AND GUN CLUB

200 West Broadway
Everglades City, FL 34139
239-695-2101
rodandguneverglades.com

The main reason to visit the Rod and Gun Club is to step back into history. This rambling, old, wooden building on the bank of the Barron River dates to the 1890s and has seen such famous guests as Ernest Hemingway and Harry Truman. I visited several times just to see the beautiful, wood-paneled lobby, bar, restaurant, and sitting rooms. The operating hours for the restaurant and bar seem to be ever-changing, sometimes due to the season. The rooms in the main lodge are not for rent, but there are several neat and clean cabins. One word of caution: When mosquitoes decide to visit the hotel grounds, you best have plenty of insect repellent.

94 SHARK VALLEY TRAM TOURS

Shark Valley Loop Road
Miami, FL 33194; 305-221-8455
sharkvalleytramtours.com

Shark Valley is in Everglades National Park about 40 miles west of downtown Miami. The way I have enjoyed this place in the past is with a self-guided bicycle tour, using my own bike. The 15-mile paved road is an easy ride because it's flat, though it's unnerving sometimes if too many gators are napping beside the path. The ride takes 2 or 3 hours or longer, depending on how often you stop. You can also rent a bicycle from Shark

SHARK VALLEY OBSERVATION TOWER, EVERGLADES NATIONAL PARK, MIAMI

Valley Tram Tours. Another great way to see things is on the 2-hour Everglades Tram Tour through this section of Everglades National Park. It's a guided tour conducted by an experienced naturalist. The tour is in an open vehicle, so you get a great view of wildlife and habitat. Halfway through the tour, you will come to a 45-foot-high observation platform that gives you a fantastic view of the Everglades. On a clear day, you can see 20 miles in all directions. Shark Valley is busiest December 26–April 25. Reservations are highly recommended during this period.

95 SMALLWOOD STORE

360 Mamie Street
Chokoloskee, FL 34138; 239-695-2989
smallwoodstore.com

Smallwood Store is one of the most historic places in southwest Florida. It is on the National Register of Historic Places. It is located on Chokoloskee Island, which is connected to Everglades City by a long causeway. The store was opened by Ted Smallwood in 1906 as a general store and trading post serving the Indigenous Seminoles and early white settlers in the area. The building perches on stilts over the edge of the water on Chokoloskee Bay at the south end of the island. It has been opened and shut over the years, sometimes due to hurricane damage. The store is open now and still looks like what it was: an Old Florida trading post, stocking items that Ted Smallwood himself would recognize. It has no air-conditioning, but when the door is open, a nice breeze flows through. It has now survived six hurricanes. Smallwood's is open 7 days a week. From December to April, the hours are 10 a.m. to 5 p.m. From May to November, the store is open from 11 a.m. to 5 p.m.

INTERIOR OF THE SMALLWOOD STORE, CHOKOLOSKEE

CHRISTMAS BOAT PARADE, FORT LAUDERDALE

Florida festivals celebrate the art, music, and culture of the state.

With a population of more than 23 million and a geographical and cultural diversity unlike any other state, there is always something going on that you will enjoy, whether it's art, music, sports, or simply the people-watching. Some events celebrate Southern culture, especially in north and central Florida. Other activities feature Latin American or African American music, art, and culture. Whatever your interests, you can find something to love at one of our festivals.

Welcome to

FESTIVALS

Find out more about FESTIVALS

96 CALLE OCHO MUSIC FESTIVAL

Calle Ocho, between SW 12th Avenue and SW 27th Avenue
Miami, FL; 305-644-8888
(Kiwanis Club of Little Havana)
carnavalmiami.com/events/calle-ocho

I think I have been part of only one world record in my life. The Calle Ocho Music Festival is in the *Guinness World Records* book for the longest conga line in the world—119,986 people in March 1988—and I was in the line. The festival celebrates Latin culture and music for one week every March. The final event on Sunday is one of the largest street festivals or block parties in the world. On this day, about 15 blocks of the Little Havana neighborhood are blocked off to traffic and opened to pedestrians. The streets are jammed with Latin musicians and performers, and hundreds of food booths serve just about every Latin dish you can imagine. You will hear merengue, tango, salsa, reggae, and other Caribbean and South American music. Kings or queens of the festival in the past have included Desi Arnaz, Willy Chirino, Gloria Estefan, and many other star performers.

97 FIESTA OF FIVE FLAGS

125 S Alcaniz Street, Suite 1
Pensacola, FL 32502; 850-433-6512
fiestapensacola.org

Pensacola is known as the City of Five Flags. It was founded in 1559 by Spanish Conquistador Don Tristan de Luna and was the first European settlement in what is now the United States. Since then, the flags of four more nations have flown over Pensacola: French, British, Confederate, and American. Although Pensacola is older than St. Augustine, St. Augustine claims the title of oldest continuously occupied city in the United States. This technicality doesn't dampen Pensacola's enthusiasm for its own history and heritage; rather, the Fiesta of Five Flags celebrates this heritage. Since 1950, it has been held the first two weeks in June and lasts 10 days. The festival kicks off in Seville Quarter, the historic district of Pensacola, and opening day features live music, food, flags, and decorations celebrating the diverse heritage of the city. Spectators can observe many parades, musical performances, art-and-sculpture contests, and the de Luna Landing Ceremony. People enjoy the festivities from both land and sea.

98 FLORIDA FOLK FESTIVAL

Stephen Foster Folk Culture Center State Park
11016 Lillian Saunders Drive,
White Springs, FL 32096
386-397-4331
floridastateparks.org/floridafolkfestival

If you love history and music, the Florida Folk Festival is a must-see. It takes place every Memorial Day weekend at Stephen Foster Folk Culture Center State Park on the Suwannee River near White Springs. You will see exhibits showing how Floridian pioneers lived and survived in the harsh environment that existed in the days before mosquito control and air-conditioning. At the three-day event, you will hear storytellers, well-known Floridian musicians, fiddle tunes, and other music brought to Florida by many generations of immigrants that have made the state their home. There are usually about 300 musical performances over the three-day weekend. Hundreds of vendors and artists have their Florida-themed wares on display, and good food is for sale all around the park, including collard greens, cornbread, chicken perlo, shrimp gumbo, and hoppin' John (a Southern dish made with rice and beans). The state park itself is also an attraction, offering 45 campsites and other amenities. If you want to spend the weekend in the area, you can find more campgrounds and motels in nearby White Springs, Lake City, Jasper, Jennings, and Live Oak.

99 GASPARILLA PIRATE FESTIVAL

Tampa Bay and downtown Tampa
gasparillapiratefest.com

Celebrated every year since 1904, this festival usually takes place in late January or early February. Its highlight is an "invasion" of downtown Tampa by a 137-foot "pirate ship" named *Jose Gasparilla* and its motley crew of pirates. Tampa Bay and the Hillsborough River turn into a floating armada of pirates and citizens having a great old time. The event celebrates José Gaspar, the legendary pirate who is said to have roamed the waters of southwest Florida. Gaspar was probably fictional, but the celebrants of this festival don't care one way or the other. The festival is a Tampa institution with deep cultural and historical roots. When the ship reaches Tampa, the mayor presents the key to the city to the captain of Ye Mystic Krewe of Gasparilla, an old organization that many Tampans are proud to belong to and that has sponsored the festival for years. Some of the members descend from the crew that held the first festival in 1904. This presentation is followed by a parade with marching bands and drill teams on Bayshore Boulevard.

100 MUG RACE

133 Crystal Cove Drive
Palatka, FL 32177; 904-264-4094
(Rudder Club of Jacksonville)
rudderclub.com

This is an unusual race you can participate in or enjoy watching. Billed as the world's longest river race for sailboats, the Mug Race starts in Palatka at 7 a.m. on the first Saturday of May and runs north for 38 nautical miles on the St. Johns River to the Buckman Bridge in Orange Park. Boats are divided into classes, and no boat can have a mast higher than 44 feet because of the clearance of one of the bridges along the route. Multihull boats start first, followed by monohull ones. Boats cannot use their engines. The fastest any boat has ever made the trip is just under 3 hours, but typical times are much longer, sometimes 12 hours or more, depending on the wind and stamina of the sailors. Some boats don't finish. This is Florida: Some days are windy, some are not. If you have a boat with an outboard motor, it's fun to watch the race from the water. There are also vantage points along the banks of the St. Johns River where you can watch the fleet go by. The first Mug Race was held in 1957. It is sponsored by the Rudder Club of Jacksonville.

101 SILVER SPURS RODEO

**Osceola Heritage Park/
Silver Spurs Arena
1875 Silver Spur Lane,
Kissimmee, FL 34744
321-697-3495
silverspursrodeo.com**

You will be close to the action during this historic rodeo, the largest east of the Mississippi River. It's fun to attend for the exciting entertainment and the link to Floridian history. The original Silver Spurs rodeo was held in 1944, when the Florida Cracker culture was strong, cattle was king, and the ranches needed lots of cowboys to work the business. This rodeo is a celebration of those Old Florida days. You will see bull riding, bronco busting, barrel racing, calf roping, and other events. The rodeo is held on the third weekend in February in the Silver Spurs Arena, part of the 150-acre Osceola Heritage Park on US 192 east of Kissimmee. The arena seats more than 11,000.

102 SUNFEST

**Flagler Drive from Banyan Boulevard
to Lakeview Avenue
West Palm Beach, FL; 561-659-5980
sunfest.com**

You will want to be a part of Florida's largest waterfront music-and-art festival. Every year more than 130,000 people crowd into downtown West Palm Beach for the event, which takes place Thursday–Sunday of the first week in May on Flagler Drive along the Intracoastal Waterway in the West Palm Beach Arts and Entertainment District. Musical groups that have performed in the past include Keith Urban, the B-52s, Flo Rida, Lil Wayne, Pit Bull, the Preservation Hall Jazz Band, Hootie and the Blowfish, and Ziggy Marley. Arts and crafts from more than 80 vendors are also displayed. Exhibits include jewelry, painting, pottery, ceramics, photography, sculpture, and wood. The grand finale of the weekend is a fireworks show on Sunday evening.

IN THE CHUTE, SILVER SPURS RODEO, KISSIMMEE

103 WINTERFEST BOAT PARADE

Corporate Headquarters
512 NE Third Avenue
Fort Lauderdale, Florida 33301
954-767-0686
winterfestparade.com

I never get tired of the Winterfest Boat Parade, an annual event held every December in Fort Lauderdale. All kinds of boats, from those just 20 feet long to mega yachts, are dressed up in lights and decorations and cruise along the New River and Intracoastal Waterway. The parade begins at 6:30 p.m., when all the boats gather along the New River downtown. The parade route runs a total of 12 miles to Pompano Beach. The extravagantly lighted vessels quite often also have musical groups aboard. One way to watch the parade is to wrangle a ride on one of the parade boats or find a friend with a boat who is willing to follow the parade. There are also plenty of spots along the river and waterway to watch, but get there early. Several waterfront restaurants and bars along the route have seating with a view, and this is my favorite way to watch: comfortably seated in a friendly watering hole (you can find a list of waterfront restaurants on the above website). Make reservations weeks in advance, however. There is also a grandstand viewing area inside Hugh Taylor Birch State Park north of Sunrise Boulevard.

104 WORM GRUNTIN' FESTIVAL

Town center, 1 block off US 319
Sopchoppy, FL 32358
wormgruntinfestival.com

Old-timers may remember Charles Kuralt of the *CBS News Sunday Morning* show. Back in 1972, he participated in worm grunting in Sopchoppy, a tiny town about 33 miles south of Tallahassee, and I watched it on TV. In later years, Mike Rowe featured it on his show *Dirty Jobs*. Sopchoppy has held the annual Worm Gruntin' Festival to showcase their skills since 2000. Worm gruntin' (Sopchoppy folks leave off the g) is a technique for drawing worms out of the ground so they can be scooped up and used for fish bait. It involves driving a wooden stake into the ground and rubbing it with a piece of iron to make it vibrate. This makes worms crawl up to the surface because they think the sound is made by moles digging (their natural predator). Some folks use a hand saw; others prefer an old leaf spring from a car. You and your kids can participate if you'd like. The event, held on the second Saturday in April, also has arts-and-crafts vendors and food booths to keep you busy, and the live music will keep your toes tapping. Admission is free.

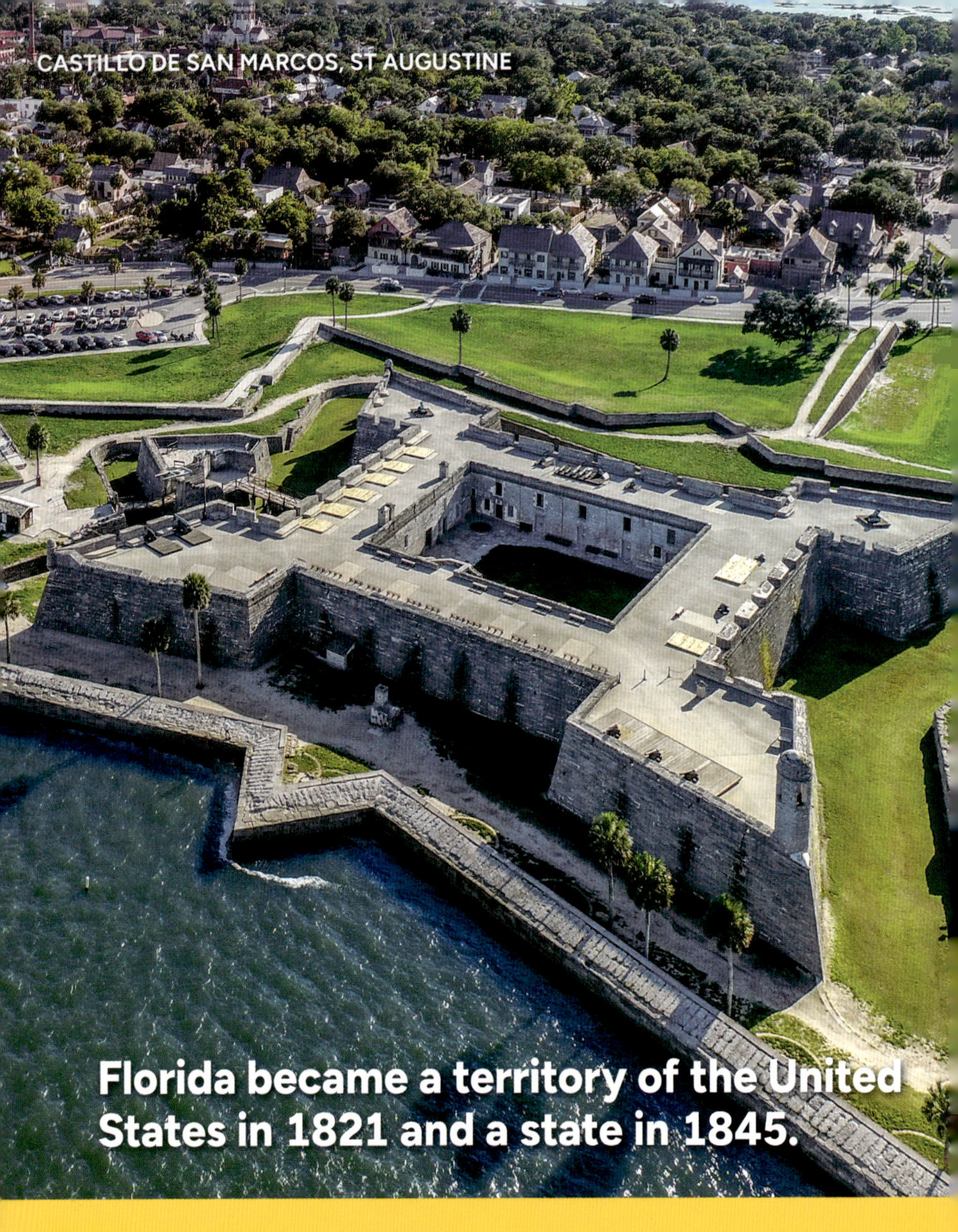

Florida became a territory of the United States in 1821 and a state in 1845.

Indigenous people were in Florida at least 14,000 years ago, but written records date back to when Juan Ponce de León arrived in 1513. Spain built the original Pensacola settlement in 1559 and founded St. Augustine in 1565, then governed Florida for most of the next 250 years. It was the third state to secede in the Civil War. Much of Florida heritage derives from the Old South, especially in north Florida. World War II spurred major economic development after its mild climate made the state a major military training center. Tourists began visiting, and to this day, many stay.

Welcome to FLORIDA HISTORY

Find out more about FLORIDA HISTORY

105 THE BARNACLE HISTORIC STATE PARK

3485 Main Highway
Miami, FL 33133; 305-442-6866
floridastateparks.org/parks-and-trails/barnacle-historic-state-park

This park is on Biscayne Bay in the historic Miami neighborhood of Coconut Grove. The Barnacle was the home of pioneer Ralph Middleton Munroe, who preserved the natural areas on his home site, cutting out only a narrow trail through the surrounding hillock. He built the home in 1891, and today's park looks the way it did when Munroe lived here. He was a sailor and boat designer, and the park even contains replicas of two of his boats. The park is for simple relaxation: picnics, walking on the paths, or rocking in a chair on the front porch with views of the bay.

106 CASTILLO DE SAN MARCOS

1 South Castillo Drive
St. Augustine, FL 32084
904-829-6506
nps.gov/casa

The Castillo dominates the waterfront and is the oldest structure in St. Augustine, completed by Spain in 1695. It sits on a 20-acre site and is the oldest 17th-century fort in North America. The fort has also been occupied by England, the Confederate States of America, and the US. Indigenous people, Minorcans, and African Americans also had roles in the fort's history. Your self-guided tour of the fort includes walking on and around the historic walls, reading the many exhibits, looking at the cannons, visiting the different rooms and learning about their functions, and reading about the history and culture of the various groups who are part of the fort's history. There are also guided tours.

107 CRACKER COUNTRY RURAL HISTORY MUSEUM

4800 US 301 North
Tampa, FL 33610; 813-627-4225
crackercountry.org

This attraction is open to the general public only during the Florida State Fair in February. A living-history museum located on the Florida State Fairgrounds in Tampa, Cracker Country features 13 buildings that were originally erected across the state between 1870 and 1912. The structures range from public buildings, like a general store and a train depot, to private spaces, such as pioneer homes. All have been decorated to display the lifestyle of the Florida pioneers, who were called Crackers. Costumed interpreters enhance this educational experience. Group tours can be arranged when the fair is not operating.

108 FORT CAROLINE NATIONAL MEMORIAL

12713 Fort Caroline Road
Jacksonville, FL 32225; 904-641-7155
nps.gov/timu/learn/historyculture/foca.htm

This memorial, on a bluff on the south bank of the St. Johns River in Jacksonville, is dedicated to the French people who settled in Florida briefly in the 1500s. France and Spain struggled for control of Florida in the 16th century, and this fort was France's foothold in the New World. Exhibits explain the history of the fort and its role in various religious and territorial disputes, as well as the first interactions between Europeans and Indigenous people. The settlement at Fort Caroline did not survive beyond its first year. Spanish troops marched up from St. Augustine and destroyed it and most of its people. This site hosts the visitor center for the entire Timucuan Preserve, which includes Fort Caroline and Kingsley Plantation.

109 FORT CHRISTMAS HISTORICAL PARK

1300 Fort Christmas Road
Christmas, FL 32709; 407-254-9310
tinyurl.com/ftchristmas

The original Fort Christmas was built on Christmas Day 1837 during the Second Seminole Indian War. The fort you will visit is a full-scale replica that includes not only Seminole and pioneer artifacts but also weapons, clothing, tools, and other items. The park grounds also include some restored Florida Cracker houses and other buildings furnished with period pieces. The park has playgrounds, picnic areas, and a small museum and hosts several events during the year. Your visit will also include a video presentation of the history of the Seminole Indian Wars.

FORT CHRISTMAS, CHRISTMAS

ENLISTED MEN'S BARRACKS, FORT CLINCH STATE PARK, AMELIA ISLAND

110 FORT CLINCH STATE PARK

2601 Atlantic Avenue
Fernandina Beach, FL 32034
904-277-7274
floridastateparks.org/fortclinch

This state park combines Florida's natural beauty and a historic fort all in one setting. The 1,400-acre park has 3 miles of shoreline on the northern end of Amelia Island. The beaches on St. Marys Inlet and the Atlantic Ocean attract shellers, anglers, and campers. The park includes miles of oak-canopied trails perfect for hiking or biking. A visit to historic Fort Clinch includes talking to park staffers dressed as uniformed soldiers reenacting life during the Civil War. You can also explore the fort's many rooms and grounds. On the first weekend of every month, the fort has a staff of uniformed soldiers who demonstrate wartime skills such as carpentry, masonry, cooking, blacksmithing, and cannon firings.

111 KINGSLEY PLANTATION

11676 Palmetto Avenue
Jacksonville, FL 32226; 904-251-3537 or 904-251-3626
nps.gov/timu/learn/historyculture/kp.htm

Kingsley Plantation is located on Fort George Island on the Fort George River in Jacksonville. It is part of the Timucuan Preserve, which also encompasses the Fort Caroline National Memorial. The plantation was the estate of Zephaniah Kingsley, the owner of several plantations in Florida. On display at this park are the owner's house, probably built around 1798 and considered to be the oldest surviving plantation house in Florida. The park also includes the remains of 25 slave cabins that were still being used after the Civil War. The grounds of the park are open to the public daily, but tours of the plantation house are allowed only by reservation on a limited basis due to ongoing preservation efforts.

112 KORESHAN STATE PARK

3800 Corkscrew Road
Estero, FL 33928; 239-992-0311
floridastateparks.org/parks-and-trails/koreshan-state-park

Florida has always had a reputation for attracting unusual people, and the Koreshan Unity was certainly unusual. This cult, whose members believed that the universe was contained within the Earth, settled in what is now Koreshan State Park. They prospered for years but died out because they all took a vow of chastity. The few elderly survivors donated their 305-acre site to the state. The grounds are loaded with natural Florida vegetation and include many gardens and exotic groves from when the Koreshans owned the land. The site includes 11 historic buildings with exhibits that explain the cult's beliefs. There are also several campsites throughout the park.

113 OLUSTEE BATTLEFIELD HISTORIC STATE PARK

5815 Battlefield Trail Road
Olustee, FL 32087; 386-758-0400
floridastateparks.org/parks-and-trails/olustee-battlefield-historic-state-park

Although Florida escaped most of the major devastation caused in the South by the Civil War, it was the site of at least one significant battle. For five hours, 10,000 men, including the 54th Massachusetts Infantry Regiment of the United States Colored Troops, waged a battle in the woods near Olustee. At the end of the day, there were 2,807 casualties, and the Union troops had retreated to Jacksonville. The battlefield became the state's first historical site. You can use the picnic area and take a mile-long walk along an interpretative trail. The park has a visitor center with exhibits and artifacts from the battle, a reenactment of which is held every February.

114 STEPHEN FOSTER FOLK CULTURE CENTER STATE PARK

11016 Lillian Saunders Drive (US 41)
White Springs, FL 32096
386-397-4331
floridastateparks.org/parks-and-trails/stephen-foster-folk-culture-center-state-park

This park honors the American composer Stephen Foster, who wrote what is now Florida's official state song, "Old Folks at Home." This song made the Suwannee River famous, and the banks of the river are a logical place for this center. The museum contains exhibits about the composer's most famous songs, and many of them can be heard from the park's 97-bell carillon during the day. You can visit the gift shop and watch demonstrations of quilting, blacksmithing, and stained-glass making. The park also has miles of trails and a campground. The Florida Folk Festival is held here every Memorial Day Weekend.

STEPHEN FOSTER STATE PARK, WHITE SPRINGS

MORIKAMI JAPANESE GARDEN WATERFALL, DELRAY BEACH

Florida's mild-to-tropical climate makes it ideal for growing a large variety of plants.

The huge population explosion in recent state history makes these botanical gardens even more attractive. They are peaceful oases that provide refuge and quiet in the busy state of Florida.

Welcome to GARDENS, FLOWERS & ARBORETUMS

115 BONNET HOUSE MUSEUM & GARDENS

900 North Birch Road
Fort Lauderdale, FL 33304
954-563-5393
bonnethouse.org

Bonnet House is a 35-acre estate on the heavily developed Fort Lauderdale Beach oceanfront and is listed on the National Register of Historic Places. The main house is full of furniture and art from the collections of the families who lived there over the years. The grounds include one of the few remaining native barrier island habitats in south Florida. Five different ecosystems are represented, and complementing the natural flora is a desert garden composed of arid plants, a hibiscus garden, and a courtyard planted with tropical vegetation. There are many orchids in this garden, and various specimens are on view at the Orchid Display House. Migratory birds find refuge at Bonnet House, and occasionally even manatees will come into the estate's Boathouse Canal.

116 FAIRCHILD TROPICAL BOTANIC GARDEN

10901 Old Cutler Road
Coral Gables, FL 33156; 305-667-1651
fairchildgarden.org

This 83-acre garden is considered to be one of the world's best tropical botanical gardens. It has extensive collections of rare tropical plants and one of the largest collections of palms in the world. You will become immersed in tropical beauty as you walk along the many paths and enjoy the displays. It is much more than a tourist attraction. It is one of the leading conservation and educational facilities in the world. Fairchild is heavily supported by the community with over 45,000 members and 1,200 volunteers who work in the gardens. And you'll definitely see orchids: Fairchild is the home of the American Orchid Society.

117 LEU GARDENS

1920 North Forest Avenue
Orlando, FL 32803; 407-246-2620
leugardens.org

The Harry P. Leu Gardens are located in north Orlando on 50 acres of some of the most beautiful botanical gardens in Florida. It has been a popular attraction since 1961, when it was donated to the city by the Leu family. The property is divided into more than 10 garden areas connected by sidewalks so that you can enjoy self-guided tours. The variety of plants is amazing and includes bananas, bromeliads, birds of paradise, cacti, bamboos, herbs, citruses, and vegetables. Some of their vegetable harvest goes to local food banks, and some is used in cooking classes that are held on the property in the Garden House.

118 MARIE SELBY BOTANICAL GARDENS

900 S. Palm Avenue
Sarasota, FL 34236; 941-366-5731
selby.org

This botanical garden spans 45 acres, with two campuses: one that is 15 acres and one that is 30 acres. Their Sarasota campus is unique, as it is the only botanical garden in the world that is dedicated to epiphytes, or plants that grow on the surface of other plants. Marie Selby also focuses on orchids and bromeliads. The gardens feature more than 20,000 living plants, including 5,500 orchids, 3,500 bromeliads, and 1,600 other plants. There are also banyans, bamboos, live oaks, palms, mangoes, succulents, wildflowers, cycads, a butterfly garden, a scent garden, and an interactive children's rainforest garden. The original gardens are located on the former estate of Marie and William Selby of the Selby Oil and Gas Company.

119 MORIKAMI MUSEUM AND JAPANESE GARDENS

4000 Morikami Park Road
Delray Beach, FL 33446; 561-495-0233
morikami.org

The Morikami Museum and Japanese Gardens has Japanese cultural exhibits that educate and inspire visitors. The history of this attraction has its roots in the Yamato Colony, a small community of Japanese pioneers who lived near Boca Raton and Delray Beach in the early 1900s. The museum building is modeled after a Japanese villa and has exhibition rooms surrounding a courtyard with a small rock garden. The building also has a 226-seat theater, an authentic tea house, and a café. The 16-acre grounds around the museum include Japanese gardens with walking paths, rest areas, and a large bonsai collection. The entire park contains 200 acres and has nature trails, pine forests, and picnic areas.

120 NAPLES BOTANICAL GARDEN

4820 Bayshore Drive
Naples, FL 34112; 239-643-7275
naplesgarden.org

This garden has been called "Gardens with Latitude" because the focus is on collections and habitats representative of plants that exist between the latitudes of 26° north and 26° south. The garden features plants from all over the world that grow within this zone. The exhibits are arranged in several gardens that include Asian, Brazilian, Caribbean, Children's, Florida, and Water. The Chabraja Visitor Center contains Kathryn's Garden, Irma's Garden (chosen for captivating colors), and LaGrippe Orchid Garden. There is also a 90-acre nature preserve with several native Floridian habitats where you can see eagles, otters, tree frogs, and gopher tortoises in their natural settings.

121 SUNKEN GARDENS

1825 Fourth Street North
St. Petersburg, FL 33704; 727-551-3102
sunkengardens.org

Sunken Gardens is a century-old botanical garden in the middle of busy, urban St. Petersburg. You will enjoy winding paths surrounded by exotic plants from all regions of the world. You can also sign up for garden tours, horticultural programs, and special events. Your tour will take you past cascading waterfalls, demonstration gardens, and more than 50,000 tropical plants and birds. Some recent special events included Frogs and Toads in the Garden, Colorful Caladiums!, and Easy Natives and Wildflowers. When you check into the gardens, you will be provided with a map that gives you details on the various plants. Parking is free.

COLUMBIA RESTAURANT, YBOR CITY IN TAMPA

Travelers from all over visit The Sunshine State for its laid-back beach bars, variety of cuisines, and nightlife.

Reliable sources claim that Florida has about 40,000 restaurants, wineries, bars, diners, and other establishments to enjoy good spirits and good times. We scratch the surface here with some of the oldest and most popular establishments. You can enjoy a wide variety of food, drinks, and entertainment at these places.

Welcome to

GOOD SPIRITS & GOOD TIMES

Columbia Restaurant in the Ybor City neighborhood of Tampa is the oldest restaurant in Florida. It opened in 1905.

A LIZARD SUNNING AT SCHNEBLY REDLAND'S WINERY, HOMESTEAD

Find out more about GOOD SPIRITS & GOOD TIMES

122 ALABAMA JACK'S

58000 Card Sound Road
Key Largo, FL 33037; 305-248-8741
facebook.com/realalabamajacks

When you are traveling to the Florida Keys down US 1, there are only two ways to get there. One is to turn left (southeast) on Card Sound Road after leaving Homestead. This takes you through mangrove swamps to a bridge that crosses Card Sound onto north Key Largo. Alabama Jack's is on the right side of the road just before the bridge. It is a typical, old waterfront restaurant. There is a nice bar inside and plenty of indoor and outdoor seating. They have good seafood, including grouper sandwiches, a grilled dolphin platter, crab cake sandwiches, and conch fritters. You don't go here as much for the food as for the experience. The bar serves great margaritas, and there are lots of beer, wine, and liquor choices. They often have live music in the Jimmy Buffett style.

123 BERN'S STEAK HOUSE

1208 South Howard Avenue
Tampa, FL 33606; 813-251-2421
bernssteakhouse.com

When I lived in Tampa, I always took my out-of-town visitors to Bern's. It is one of the earliest examples of farm-to-table restaurants in Florida. In Bern's case, the restaurant owns its own farm, so the chefs know exactly what they are serving. They are famous for their perfectly aged steaks. My personal favorite is their 6-ounce filet mignon. Boasting one of the largest wine collections in the world, Bern's invites guests to take a tour of the huge wine cellar and kitchen. Bern's also has an internationally famous dessert room. Although I am usually not a dessert person, I always visit this room and usually select a King Midas spiced carrot cake to finish off my meal. These features have made Bern's a local favorite since 1956.

124 CAP'S PLACE ISLAND RESTAURANT

2765 NE 28th Court (Dock Location)
Lighthouse Point, FL 33064
954-941-0418
capsplace.com

Historic Cap's Place was built in 1928 and is an Old Florida icon that should be visited at least once by everyone interested in Floridian history. It is on the National Register of Historic Places. People go to Cap's for the ambience. Many famous visitors have dined and imbibed here, including Joe DiMaggio, Jack Dempsey, and Myrna Loy. Cap's is on the tip of a residential peninsula. You get there by a 5-minute boat ride that operates out of Lighthouse Point marina. The walls of the restaurant are filled with photos and newspaper clippings of the old days. Cap's overlooks the water with views of yachts, mansions, and shoreline mangroves. The menu specializes in fresh fish, scallops, crab cakes, shrimp dishes, and lobster. They also have hearts-of-palm salad (known as swamp cabbage) and Key lime pie.

125 THE CHATTAWAY

358 22nd Avenue South
St. Petersburg, FL 33705; 727-823-1594
thechattaway.com

This Old Florida establishment has been serving casual diners in St. Petersburg since 1951. It features outdoor dining and is a favorite of the locals. Tourists have a bit harder time finding it because it is a little south of the downtown district of marinas and museums. A distinctive feature of the decor is the ubiquitous claw-foot bathtubs, which are used as planters for exotic flowers and tropical plants. The most famous dish here is the 7-ounce hamburger loaded with everything you want and named the Chattaburger. There are other sandwiches, seafood entrées, salads, and soups, as well, and they also serve beer and wine.

126 CLUB CONTINENTAL

2143 Astor Street
Orange Park, FL 32073; 800-877-6070
clubcontinental.com

Club Continental, located in Orange Park along the St. Johns River, has been a cherished dining and social destination since its origins as a private estate in the 1920s, with the current club established in the mid-20th century. Built as the winter retreat of Caleb Johnson (of Palmolive Soap fame), the Mediterranean Revival mansion was transformed into a private club in 1966; its River House Pub and dining facilities have since made the club a local favorite. Reservations are recommended, especially for non-members, as it retains a semi-private club feel. There are also 22 guest rooms available to non-members. Dress code is country club casual: collared shirts and slacks, no jeans or T-shirts.

127 COLUMBIA RESTAURANT

2117 East Seventh Avenue
Tampa, FL 33605; 813-248-4961
columbiarestaurant.com

My first job after graduating from college was in Tampa. My boss took my wife and me to the Columbia, and it was one of the most fantastic experiences I have ever had. Taking up an entire Ybor City block, it is one of the largest Spanish restaurants in the world, seating 1,700 in 15 dining rooms. The interior architecture is breathtaking. The oldest restaurant in Florida, the Columbia was founded in 1905 by Cuban immigrant Casimiro Hernandez Sr. and is still operated by his descendants. The food is delicious Spanish and Cuban cuisine, and the sangria and other drinks are great. They have a 50,000-bottle wine inventory. The entertainment is also fabulous, featuring a world-class flamenco show. The Columbia's success has led to several other operations around Florida featuring the name, but this location is the original and, in my opinion, the best.

128 HENSCRATCH FARMS VINEYARD AND WINERY

980 Henscratch Road
Lake Placid, FL 33852; 863-699-2060
henscratchfarms.com

Henscratch Farms Vineyard and Winery is unique in that it is also a small working farm. Two hundred hens have free range under the canopy of the vineyard. Several breeds of laying hens wander the property, but one makes me think of the children's author Dr. Seuss. The Aracaunas lay large green eggs. Remember the silly book about green eggs and ham? The winery's small country store is built in the old-fashioned Florida Cracker style. Inside, you will find many types of wines, jams, jellies, sauces, and syrups. Products vary with the harvest season. Strawberry preserves, blueberry dressing, and jams and jellies are displayed on the tasting counter, so you can try a sample and sip some wine. They also sell eggs along with raw honey from their own hives.

129 HIGH TIDES AT SNACK JACK

2805 S. Oceanshore Boulevard
Flagler Beach, FL 32136; 386-439-3344
snackjacks.com

Snack Jack has been at this beachfront location since 1947. It is directly on the ocean, and every booth or table has a view of the rolling surf. There is also outside dining. The menu, of course, is loaded with seafood dishes, including platters, conch fritters, tacos, sandwiches, and salads. The kitchen knows how to steam, grill, blacken, and prepare all kinds of food the way you like, including the good old frying method. The minute you walk inside the rambling, rustic building, you will feel as though you've been transported to a surfing museum. The walls and ceilings are festooned with all kinds of interesting objects, including surfboards. The main dining room also has a small bar where you can eat or just have a drink. Don't dress up to go to Snack Jack. T-shirt, shorts, and flip-flops are always in style here.

130 JOE'S STONE CRAB

11 Washington Avenue
Miami Beach, FL 33139; 305-673-0365
joesstonecrab.com

When I lived on my boat in Miami Beach, a favorite evening tradition was a stroll to nearby Joe's Stone Crab for drinks and dinner. The restaurant was opened in 1913 by Joe Weiss. After all these years, Joe's is still the top buyer of Floridian stone-crab claws, their most famous dish. Joe's is frequented by the rich and famous, but I used to go there, so you can too. The servers are professionals, and many of their fathers and grandfathers also worked at Joe's. The maître d' is king. They take no reservations, so you approach him and give him your name and the size of your party. You might give him a tip at this point, and I don't mean "buy low and sell high." Then you will wait, but the wait is a lot of fun, especially at the bar. Although there are many other items on the menu, if you come for stone crabs, remember they are seasonal and must be cooked the day they are caught. The best time to go is during the season, from October 15 to May 15. Prices vary by harvest and amount.

131 LAKERIDGE WINERY & VINEYARDS

19239 US 27 North
Clermont, FL 34715; 800-768-9463
lakeridgewinery.com

This winery has become a popular Orlando-area attraction. The beautiful main building and vineyards are on a 127-acre estate in the hilly country about 25 miles west of Orlando. The vineyard takes up 77 acres and includes Florida-hybrid bunch grapes and varieties of muscadines. The winery has a large tasting room and an attractive gift shop. Several types of wine are sold under the Lakeridge brands. In addition to the wines, the gift shop sells gourmet foods, cheeses, crackers, sauces, and wine accessories. There are probably more events held at this establishment than at any other Florida winery. All year long, there are arts-and-crafts shows, jazz concerts, harvest festivals, grape-stomping events, vintage car shows, and vintage music events. Complimentary tours and wine tastings are offered daily.

132 MAI-KAI RESTAURANT

3599 North Federal Highway
Fort Lauderdale, FL 33308
954-563-3272
maikai.com

Mai-Kai is a Polynesian-themed restaurant and nightclub that opened in 1956 and is on the National Register of Historic Places and has recently been renovated. When you step inside, you feel as though you are in a tropical place on some South Sea island. The extensive menu includes duck, beef, chicken, pork, seafood, and vegetarian selections. All food is prepared with Asian spices using Asian cooking techniques. The drinks are huge, and it takes only one to get you in the mood for the Polynesian stage show you will enjoy after dinner. Dancers show their stuff to fantastic drum beats with lots of fiery torches. Dress up a little bit: no T-shirts and baggy shorts. No coat and tie required, but wear a shirt with a collar and some nice shorts or slacks.

MAI-KAI RESTAURANT, FORT LAUDERDALE

133 SAN SEBASTIAN WINERY

157 King Street
St. Augustine, FL 32084
904-826-1594
sansebastianwinery.com

This winery has been in business since 1996 and is the second-largest winery in Florida. Over 160,000 visitors a year come to taste wine and tour the 18,0000-square-foot facility, which has a gourmet gift shop and a storage capacity of 40,000 gallons of wine. Besides the wines, you can purchase domestic and imported beers, as well as appetizers. Native varieties of Noble (red) and Carlos and Welder (white) muscadines are grown for the winery by Lakeridge Winery Estate and Prosperity Vineyards. There is an open-air deck on the second floor, where you can enjoy your wine and snacks while listening to music. The view of St. Augustine is wonderful from the deck, and music is provided every weekend.

134 SCHNEBLY REDLAND'S WINERY

30205 SW 217th Avenue
Homestead, FL 33030; 305-242-1224
schneblywinery.com

Schnebly Redland's Winery is noted not just for its exotic wine but also for its entertaining and comfortable venue. The winery makes delicious wines out of all kinds of tropical fruits. The Redland is a large agricultural area that gets its name from the red clay soil that dominates the area. Exotic plants and vegetables that will not grow anywhere else in the United States thrive in the soil here. The winery's 30 acres of tropical fruits include carambola, mango, lychee, guava, passion fruit, and gourmet vegetables. The buildings and grounds are beautifully maintained, and there are a couple of fountains and waterfalls located among the lush tropical plantings that surround the building. The retail store and wine-tasting areas are up front.

135 SLOPPY JOE'S BAR

201 Duval Street
Key West, FL 33040; 305-294-5717
sloppyjoes.com

Sloppy Joe's Bar has long been a part of the quirky nature of Key West. It was a favorite hangout of Ernest Hemingway, who lived in Key West for many years. People visit the bar mainly for its historic atmosphere, but it also serves good drinks and decent food, including salads and pizza. Millions of locals and visitors have come here since it first went into business under another name in the 1930s.

THE BILTMORE, CORAL GABLES

Historic buildings offer both beauty and an opportunity to learn about the past.

The oldest buildings in Florida are in St. Augustine, reflecting the Spanish heritage dating back to 1565. Many architectural masterpieces in the rest of the state were constructed during Florida's Gilded Age of the 1880s and 1890s. Some of the most impressive buildings were built during the real estate boom of the 1920s and are still functioning as hotels or other businesses. Florida also has its share of historic mansions, many of which have been preserved and converted into museums.

Welcome to

HISTORIC BUILDINGS & ARCHITECTURE

Many Florida towns still have magnificent hotels that date back to the late 19th century, in addition to those that were built during the Florida real estate boom of the 1920s.

Find out more about

HISTORIC BUILDINGS & ARCHITECTURE

136 THE ANCIENT SPANISH MONASTERY

16711 West Dixie Highway
North Miami Beach, FL 33160
305-945-1461
spanishmonastery.com

Don't feel tricked: Although it truly is Florida's oldest building, there is a catch. The monastery was actually built in Spain in 1141. It was purchased by William Randolph Hearst, taken apart stone by stone, and shipped to America, finally ending up here in North Miami Beach. The building is more than 400 years older than some of the national historic monuments in St. Augustine. The buildings and grounds are beautiful and have become a popular place for weddings and other special ceremonies. Church services are held on Sundays.

137 ART DECO HISTORIC DISTRICT

The Art Deco Welcome Center
1001 Ocean Drive
Miami Beach, FL 33139; 305-672-2014
mdpl.org

The Miami Design Preservation League was established to protect and preserve the Art Deco buildings built in the Streamline Moderne style in Miami Beach during the Great Depression and up to the beginning of World War II. These buildings are complemented by a mix of other designs, some known as Tropical Deco. This part of Miami Beach—known as South Beach—has an interesting mix of well-preserved and functioning hotels, restaurants, and shops with Art Deco, Mediterranean Revival, and Miami Modern styles. Walking tours can be arranged, or you can explore the neighborhood on your own.

138 THE BILTMORE

1200 Anastasia Avenue
Coral Gables, FL 33134; 855-311-6903
biltmorehotel.com

The Biltmore is a luxury hotel and resort where you can spend time in magnificent surroundings. Built in 1926 in the Spanish Colonial style, it has been used as a setting for movies and television shows, including *Miami Vice*, and its swimming pool is the largest on the East Coast. The rich and famous have stayed here, including the Duke and Duchess of Windsor, President Franklin D. Roosevelt, Bing Crosby, and even the infamous Al Capone. Activities include golf and cooking classes conducted by the Biltmore Culinary Academy.

139 BOK TOWER GARDENS

1151 Tower Boulevard
Lake Wales, FL 33853; 863-676-1408
boktowergardens.org

The quiet, serene gardens of Bok Tower are a pleasant contrast to the busy activity of the theme parks in Orlando and elsewhere in central Florida. This attraction is only an hour and a half from Orlando, but it seems far away from the traffic. Edward Bok was the editor of *Ladies' Home Journal* and transformed this sandy hill near Lake Wales into one of the most beautiful places in the country. The tropical plantings shade visitors and are home to more than 125 species of birds. The singing tower with its carillon plays concerts every day at 1 p.m. and 3 p.m., plus shorter musical pieces at other times during the day. Bok Tower Gardens has also become one of Florida's most popular wedding venues.

140 THE BREAKERS

1 South County Road
Palm Beach, FL 33480; 833-777-7610
thebreakers.com

The Breakers is a 538-room hotel and resort on the Atlantic Ocean that was opened in 1896 by Florida railroad tycoon Henry Flagler. If you stay at this resort, you will be surrounded by the opulent history of Palm Beach. Many large conferences and conventions are held here, and the hotel has more than 2,000 employees. The Italian Renaissance architectural design was inspired by 15th-century Italian villas. The hotel has nine restaurants, two 18-hole golf courses, four swimming pools, and a private beach on the Atlantic Ocean.

141 CA' D'ZAN

5401 Bay Shore Boulevard
Sarasota, FL 34243; 941-359-5700
ringling.org/visit/venues/ca-dzan/

John Ringling made his fortune in the circus business. He and his brothers operated the circus known as "The Greatest Show on Earth." His personal home, Ca' d'Zan (Venetian dialect for "House of John"), is a mansion constructed in the Venetian Gothic style. In addition to the mansion, the Ringling complex includes the Museum of Art (page 15) and the Circus Museum. A museum ticket gets you into both museums but not into the mansion. You can buy a ticket that includes admission to the museums and a tour of Ca' d'Zan led by a docent. There are many tour and admission options; go to the website before visiting so you can make the right decision about what you want to see and what time you want to see it.

142 CASSADAGA SPIRITUALIST CAMP

1112 Stevens Street
Cassadaga, FL 32706; 386-228-2880
cassadaga.org

This historic town is on the National Register of Historic Places and has preserved its original roots as a spiritualist camp. There are many Victorian-era cottages and homes in the camp where the spiritualists live and work. There are many mediums in the village, and many self-proclaimed healers who pride themselves on teaching people to tap into their own ability to heal themselves. There is a hotel on-site that is reportedly home to ghosts, and there is a gift shop with crystals, stones, jewelry, DVDs and CDs, and a large collection of books on spiritualism and metaphysics.

143 CORAL CASTLE

28655 South Dixie Highway
Miami, FL 33033; 305-248-6345
coralcastle.com

Latvian Ed Leedskalnin was about to be married to his 16-year-old sweetheart when she backed out the day before the wedding. Ed was broken-hearted and left for America, ending up in Florida in 1922. He decided to create a monument to his sweetheart and started work on his castle. Ed was just over 5 feet tall and weighed 120 pounds. This fact will amaze you when you see the size of the giant rocks he used to build his monument. All by himself, he carved more than 1,000 tons of coral rock and moved the pieces into locations on his property. He had no large machinery, and he did most of his work after sunset, using lanterns for light. Each section of the wall at Coral Castle is 8 feet tall, 4 feet wide, and 3 feet thick. Ed died without ever revealing the mystery of how he was able to manipulate these giant rocks. He said only that he understood the laws of weight and leverage.

144 DEFUNIAK SPRINGS HISTORIC DISTRICT

71 US 90 West
DeFuniak Springs, FL 32433
850-892-8500
defuniaksprings.net/1170/historic-district-information

This small Panhandle city has a large collection of Victorian homes and other buildings surrounding a circular lake in the historic downtown area. The town was the summer home of the Florida Chautauqua Assembly (an educational movement) from 1885 to 1927. The DeFuniak Springs Historic District, along with several individual homes, is listed on the National Register of Historic Places.

145 FLAGLER COLLEGE (HOTEL PONCE DE LEON)

74 King Street
St. Augustine, FL 32084; 904-823-3378
legacy.flagler.edu/pages/tours

Flagler College is housed in the former Hotel Ponce de Leon. This building is a memory trip for me, as I spent a New Year's Eve as a guest in this hotel many years ago. The hotel was built by railroad tycoon Henry Flagler in 1888 and is a National Historic Landmark. You can take a tour and explore the courtyard while learning of the hotel's Spanish Renaissance architecture and of the techniques used to construct it. You will also visit the grand lobby, with its 68-foot domed ceiling supported by eight ornate oak caryatids. The dining room contains 40 Louis Comfort Tiffany stained glass windows, along with hand-painted murals on the walls and ceiling. You will also see personal photos and mementos of Henry Flagler and his family. The hotel undergoes periodic renovation, so make sure to call the college for current tour information.

EDWARD LEEDSKALNIN SECRETLY CARVED OVER 1,100 TONS OF CORAL ROCK TO FORM THIS BEAUTIFUL CORAL CASTLE, MIAMI

146 FLORIDA STATE CAPITOL

400 South Monroe Street
Tallahassee, FL 32399; 850-488-6167
floridacapitol.myflorida.com

Tallahassee became the capital of the Florida Territory back in 1824 and has held onto this distinction through statehood and beyond. The old capitol building has been preserved and restored and is next door to the modern tower that serves as the headquarters for Florida's state government. You can take a self-guided tour, the highlight of which is a trip to the 22nd-floor observation deck for a breathtaking view of Tallahassee.

147 FRANK LLOYD WRIGHT, "A CHILD OF THE SUN"

Florida Southern College
111 Lake Hollingsworth Drive
Lakeland, FL 33801; 863-680-4597
flsouthern.edu/frank-lloyd-wright-home

Florida Southern College in Lakeland is home to 13 buildings designed by Frank Lloyd Wright from 1938 to 1959 and is on the National Register of Historic Places. The structures, together referred to as "A Child of the Sun," are still used by students and faculty today. The visitor center has photographs, furniture, and drawings related to Wright's work on the campus, as well as a gift shop. Guided tours of the Wright-designed buildings are offered by appointment. You can also tour the campus on your own; be sure to purchase a map at the visitor center.

148 HENRY B. PLANT MUSEUM

401 West Kennedy Boulevard
Tampa, FL 33606; 813-254-1891
plantmuseum.com

Plant Hall, the University of Tampa's central building, once housed the Tampa Bay Hotel. Built in 1891, the resort's Moorish minarets have long been an iconic symbol of Tampa. It was built by railroad magnate Henry B. Plant as a luxury resort hotel with more than 500 rooms and hosted famous guests such as Teddy Roosevelt and Stephen Crane. The Henry B. Plant Museum is inside and contains the actual furnishings enjoyed by the first guests to visit here, reflecting the opulence of turn-of-the-20th-century America and the vision of Henry B. Plant.

149 HENRY MORRISON FLAGLER MUSEUM (WHITEHALL)

1 Whitehall Way
Palm Beach, FL 33480; 561-655-2833
flaglermuseum.us

Whitehall was the luxurious 75-room mansion of railroad tycoon Henry Flagler. When it was completed in 1902, the *New York Herald* declared it "more wonderful than any palace in Europe, grander and more magnificent than any other private dwelling in the world." Today, Whitehall is a National Historic Landmark. Now open to the public as the Henry Morrison Flagler Museum, it features tours, shifting exhibits, and special programs. Many of the original furnishings are still in the building, and there is also a large art collection.

150 OLDEST HOUSE MUSEUM COMPLEX

14 St. Francis Street
St. Augustine, FL 32084
904-824-2872
staughs.com/oldest-house-museum-complex

The Oldest House Museum Complex is located across from the historic National Guard building in downtown St. Augustine. Admission includes a guided tour of Florida's Oldest House, a museum featuring a gallery of five centuries of American maps, a changing exhibit gallery, a garden containing classic St. Augustine plants, and a museum store. The house is open from 10 a.m. to 5 p.m. daily, and tours run every half hour.

151 PENSACOLA HISTORIC VILLAGE

120 Church Street
Pensacola, FL 32502; 850-595-5985
historicpensacola.org

Historic Pensacola is a neighborhood of 28 buildings that bring to life the city's more than 450-year history. The village is managed by the University of West Florida Historic Trust and is in downtown Pensacola. The district features charming homes, museums, art galleries, restaurants, and shops. Among the properties you will see are the T. T. Wentworth Jr. Museum, Pensacola Children's Museum, the Museum of Commerce, the Museum of Industry, Old Christ Church, Tivoli High House, Dorr House, Julee Cottage, Fountain Park, and the Colonial Archaeological Trail. Both guided and self-guided tours are available.

152 SEASIDE

Scenic Highway 30A, between Panama City Beach and Destin
seasidefl.com

Seaside is a planned community created in 1981 on what had been an 80-acre private family retreat near Seagrove Beach. The community is a pioneer of the concept now known as New Urbanism. Seaside has spurred the development of similar communities in Florida and elsewhere. It was also the setting for the movie *The Truman Show*. The town is designed for pedestrians. You can park your car and wander all over town on trails and sidewalks. The houses and other buildings are modern versions typical of Old Florida architecture with wide, overhanging eaves; porches; and wood-frame construction.

153 VIZCAYA MUSEUM & GARDENS

3251 South Miami Avenue
Miami, FL 33129; 305-250-9133
vizcaya.org

The Vizcaya Museum & Gardens is the former estate of James Deering of the Deering-McCormick International Harvester fortune. It is on Biscayne Bay in the Coconut Grove neighborhood of Miami. Built in the early 20th century, the estate's landscape and architecture were influenced by Italian Renaissance designs. Vizcaya was Deering's winter residence from 1916 until his death in 1925.

154 YBOR CITY HISTORIC DISTRICT

Ybor City Visitor Information Center
1600 East 8th Avenue
Tampa, FL 33605; 813-241-8838
ybor.org

You will enjoy walking the narrow, brick streets of Ybor City and feeling its Old World charm. Known as Tampa's Latin Quarter for over a century, Ybor City is a National Historic Landmark District founded in 1886 by Don Vicente Martinez-Ybor when he moved his cigar factory from Key West to Tampa. Historic buildings have been preserved or converted to stylish offices, homes, and boutique hotels without sacrificing their historic character.

SUNSET VIEW OF BAHIA HONDA STATE PARK, BIG PINE KEY

The Keys are for people who love boating, fishing, and the unusual.

The Florida Keys are a string of coral cays that stretch from the mainland south of Miami all the way through Key West to the Dry Tortugas. Instead of sand beaches, most of these cays have shores of coral rock. The Keys are known for their geology, a culture, and a sometimes-turbulent history. In 1982, the people of Key West had a disagreement with the US government and jokingly declared their independence, briefly becoming the Conch Republic. This brought much publicity to the Keys and cemented their quirky reputation, which still sticks today.

Welcome to THE KEYS

155 BAHIA HONDA STATE PARK 80

Big Pine Key

Stop here 30 miles before Key West for great views, activities, and camping.

156 DOLPHIN CONNECTION 80

Duck Key

Since 1990, this attraction has been training dolphins and educating people about these amazing animals.

157 THE ERNEST HEMINGWAY HOME & MUSEUM 80

Key West

The famous author lived here, and you can still visit with the descendants of his six-toed cats.

158 HARRY S. TRUMAN LITTLE WHITE HOUSE 81

Key West

The 33rd president of the United States made this his winter home for a total of 175 days.

159 KEY WEST AQUARIUM 81

Key West

At one time this was the world's only outdoor aquarium; it's an interesting and peaceful place to visit.

160 MALLORY SQUARE 82

Key West

Many generations of tourists and locals have gathered here to watch the entertainment and fabulous sunsets.

161 THEATER OF THE SEA 82

Islamorada

Here you can get up close to an amazing variety of animals, including birds and dolphins.

Find out more about THE KEYS

155 BAHIA HONDA STATE PARK

36850 Overseas Highway
Big Pine Key, FL 33043; 305-872-2353
floridastateparks.org/BahiaHonda

About 30 miles before you get to Key West on the Overseas Highway, you will come to Bahia Honda State Park and want to stop and linger for a few hours or a few days. The address says Big Pine Key, but the park is located on Bahia Honda Key, a largely undeveloped key with its original, natural setting. This beautiful park gives you open views of the sea from the historic Old Bahia Honda Bridge. Other activities include swimming, boating, fishing, and snorkeling. The beautiful, sandy beaches here are unusual in the coral-rimmed Keys, and the views of the sunset are amazing. The park's campground is one of the most popular in the state. You can make campsite reservations 11 months in advance, and many people do. Bahia Honda is an excellent place to see wading birds and shorebirds, while the Sand and Sea Nature Center introduces nature lovers to the island's plants and animals.

156 DOLPHIN CONNECTION

61 Hawks Cay Boulevard
Duck Key, FL 33050; 305-289-9975
dolphinconnection.com

Dolphin Connection, in business since 1990, is located at the Hawks Cay Resort. As the name implies, staff members focus on dolphins and have a worldwide reputation as experts on the bottlenose dolphin. The facility is centered on a circular saltwater lagoon. You can meet dolphins and be amazed at the obvious intelligence and good nature of these friendly mammals. The owners and employees of this facility believe in providing the highest-possible level of care to their dolphins. There are various levels of experiences available, ranging from interacting with the dolphins from a dock to getting into the water with them to the 3-hour Trainer-for-a-Day program.

157 THE ERNEST HEMINGWAY HOME & MUSEUM

907 Whitehead Street
Key West, FL 33040; 305-294-1136
hemingwayhome.com

In 1931, Key West became the home of Ernest and Pauline Hemingway. Built in 1851 in the Spanish Colonial style, their house was constructed using limestone excavated at the home site. The resulting pit created a large basement, rare in the Keys. Another rarity was the extravagant swimming pool that Hemingway built. Ernest kidded his wife about the cost of the pool, saying, "Pauline, you've spent all but my last penny, so you might as well have that!" Visitors can see that penny embedded in cement by the pool. You will probably also see some polydactyl (six-toed) cats on the property. These are the beloved and well-cared-for descendants of a polydactyl cat given to Hemingway by a visiting sea captain. The home's interior is filled with European antiques and animal trophies from Hemingway's African safaris.

HEMINGWAY'S HOUSE, KEY WEST

158 HARRY S. TRUMAN LITTLE WHITE HOUSE

111 Front Street
Key West, FL 33040; 305-509-6139
trumanlittlewhitehouse.com

This old home in the Truman Annex neighborhood is Florida's only presidential museum. Harry S. Truman, the 33rd president of the United States, loved Key West and made this house his winter White House. The home is filled with the original furniture, documents, and memorabilia from Truman's time, and guides and video presentations will tell you all about those years and before. President Truman stayed here for a total of 175 days during his presidential term, but before that the house served as the naval station's command headquarters during the Spanish-American War and World Wars I and II. Other famous residents include inventor Thomas Edison, who lived here during World War I while working on underwater weapons. The house is still used for government functions today.

159 KEY WEST AQUARIUM

1 Whitehead Street
Key West, FL 33040; 305-910-2791
keywestaquarium.com

The Key West Aquarium was built by the federal government's Works Progress Administration between 1933 and 1935. At the time of its founding, it was the world's only open-air aquarium. This is a simple aquarium without a lot of the high-tech adventures typically included in many modern, big-city establishments. One of the goals of the aquarium is to help preserve the natural habitat and animals of the Florida Keys. Contributing to that effort is the sea turtle conservation program, where injured sea turtles are rehabilitated and released. In addition to exhibits devoted to alligators, sharks, jellyfish, and stingrays, you will also see many game and reef fish, such as cobia, tarpon, angelfish, and parrotfish. Plan to spend a few relaxing hours here in this peaceful place.

160 MALLORY SQUARE

400 Wall Street
Key West, FL 33040
mallorysquare.com

From the earliest visits I made to Key West many years ago until now, the public area of Mallory Square has been the gathering place for locals and tourists to enjoy the sunset and entertainment. The square is located near the north end of Duval Street and fronts the Gulf. Its Sunset Celebration includes arts-and-crafts shows, street performers, and food carts. The sunset is still the main attraction, but you can also dine in one of the restaurants or shop in a retail outlet. One of the sights to see in Mallory Square is the Key West Historic Memorial Sculpture Garden, which contains bronze busts of people who had a major impact on the history of Key West. Joining the busts of many local, home-grown heroes are those of Henry Flagler, Ernest Hemingway, Harry S. Truman, and permanent and part-time residents.

161 THEATER OF THE SEA

84721 Overseas Highway
Islamorada, FL 33036; 305-664-2431
theaterofthesea.com

Theater of the Sea is a family-owned venture that has been in business since 1946. It is one of the oldest marine facilities in the world. The lagoons and tropical gardens are home to dolphins, sea lions, sea turtles, tropical fish, game fish, sharks, stingrays, alligators, birds, and others. You will get to observe various shows from up close involving dolphins, sea lions, parrots, and other animals. There are also many interactive programs, such as swimming with a sea lion or a dolphin. You can get close for a view of sea turtles and even alligators. Attractions include a bottomless boat ride, a fish and reptile tour, walking on a lagoon beach, and much more. The dolphin swims last 30 minutes and include dorsal tows, hugs, and swimming and snorkeling.

THEATER OF THE SEA, ISLAMORADA

BOCA GRANDE LIGHTHOUSE (1890), GASPARILLA ISLAND, BOCA GRANDE

Florida's lighthouses offer a unique blend of history, architecture, and gorgeous views of sea and shore.

Lighthouses in the Sunshine State are among its oldest structures and make entertaining destinations for Florida day trips. All of them have interesting stories to tell, and some can be visited by tourists. One of the oldest lighthouses on mainland Florida is the one in St. Augustine that was built in 1871. The tallest in Florida is at Ponce de Leon Inlet south of Daytona Beach. It is 175 feet tall and one of the tallest in the United States. Some of Florida's lighthouses allow visitors to climb to the top, and a few also serve as popular wedding locations.

Welcome to

LIGHTHOUSES

Find out more about LIGHTHOUSES

162 AMELIA ISLAND LIGHTHOUSE

**215 O'Hagan Lane
Fernandina Beach, FL 32034
(tours leave from Atlantic Recreation Center, 2500 Atlantic Avenue)
904-310-3350
fbfl.us/1097/Amelia-Island-Lighthouse**

The Amelia Island Lighthouse overlooks Egan's Creek and the St. Mary's River at its entrance to the Atlantic Ocean. Built in 1838 using materials from a lighthouse formerly located on Georgia's Cumberland Island, it is the oldest existing lighthouse in Florida. The U.S. Coast Guard transferred ownership of it to the city of Fernandina Beach in 2001, and the city now maintains it as a historical monument. Access is limited by the city as the structure is in a residential neighborhood. Lighthouse grounds are open on Saturdays from 11 a.m. to 2 p.m. Tours of the lighthouse itself are given on the first and third Wednesdays of every month at 10 a.m. Reservations are required for the tour.

163 CAPE FLORIDA LIGHT

**Bill Baggs Cape Florida State Park
1200 South Crandon Boulevard
Key Biscayne, FL 33149; 305-361-8779
floridastateparks.org/parks-and-trails/bill-baggs-cape-florida-state-park**

The Cape Florida Light is on the southern tip of Key Biscayne, southeast of Miami. Built in 1825, it is one of Florida's oldest lighthouses. It operated until 1878, when its role was replaced by a new light offshore at Fowey Rocks. In 1966, the state purchased the property that would later become Bill Baggs Cape Florida State Park, and the U.S. Coast Guard reactivated the light in 1978. It was deactivated again in 1992 because of hurricane damage and has been in operation again since 1996. The lighthouse and keeper's quarters have been restored, and the lighthouse is open to the public. Guided tours take place Thursday–Monday from 10 a.m. to 12 p.m. Climb the 95 steps of the tower for a fantastic view of Key Biscayne and Miami Beach.

164 CROOKED RIVER LIGHTHOUSE

**1975 US 98 West
Carrabelle, FL 32322; 850-697-2732
crookedriverlighthouse.org**

The Crooked River Lighthouse was built in 1895 to guide anglers, oyster harvesters, and lumber ships through the pass between Dog and St. George Islands. In 1995, the U. S. Coast Guard decommissioned the lighthouse, and it was headed for auction. A local citizens group formed the Carrabelle Lighthouse Association (CLA) to restore and preserve the lighthouse and open it to the public. The lighthouse is now owned by the city of Carrabelle, and the Keeper's House Museum is open Wednesday–Sunday. The lighthouse tower is open for climbs during daytime hours for an additional fee. All climbers must be at least 44 inches tall.

165 GASPARILLA ISLAND LIGHT

220 Gulf Boulevard
Boca Grande, FL 33921; 941-964-0060
https://www.bips.org

Originally in service as a range light in Delaware, the Gasparilla Island Light was disassembled in 1921 and put back together in 1927 on Gasparilla Island. It began service in 1932 as the rear-entrance range light for Port Boca Grande and was coordinated with the front-entrance light about 1 mile offshore (the front light was removed years ago). The Gasparilla Island Light is one of two lighthouses that can be seen today on Gasparilla Island, the other being the Port Boca Grande Lighthouse (see page 87), located in Gasparilla Island State Park to the south.

166 HILLSBORO INLET LIGHTHOUSE

907 Hillsboro Mile
Hillsboro Beach, FL 33062
954-942-2102 (museum)
hillsborolighthouse.org

The Hillsboro Lighthouse was built in 1906 and is located on the east side of Hillsboro Inlet. A museum operated by the Hillsboro Lighthouse Preservation Society is located on the west side of the inlet at 2700 N. Ocean Boulevard. A statue of the Barefoot Mailman on the lighthouse site memorializes the mail carriers who walked an 80-mile route along the beach in the late 19th century. One of the mailmen disappeared while walking the route in 1887 and was presumed to have either drowned or been killed by an alligator or shark while trying to swim across Hillsboro Inlet. The lighthouse is open periodically for tours, and you are required to take a boat from a nearby dock to visit it. You are permitted to climb the 175-step lighthouse tower on these tours. Call the museum for information on tour dates and times. The museum is now open seven days a week from 11 a.m. to 3 p.m.

167 JUPITER INLET LIGHTHOUSE

500 Captain Armour's Way
Jupiter, FL 33469; 561-747-8380
jupiterlighthouse.org

The Jupiter Inlet Lighthouse & Museum has been open to the public since 1973. The tower was first lit in 1860 and has a wonderful view of Jupiter Inlet and the Atlantic Ocean. Tours of the lighthouse grounds and museum, including tower climbs, are available to the public. The lighthouse property also serves as a park and community center for the area and has a busy event schedule. The museum features many exhibits of Indigenous and early pioneer culture. Access to the lighthouse is by paid, guided tour only, and tickets are purchased in the museum.

168 MOUNT DORA LIGHTHOUSE

Grantham Point at Gilbert Park
311 S. Tremain Street
Mount Dora, FL 32757
fl-mountdora.civicplus.com/facilities/facility/details/gilbert-park-7

The Mount Dora Lighthouse is considered by many purists not to be the real thing—a faux lighthouse, so to speak. The lighthouse is only 35 feet tall and is not open to the public. It is, however, an official registered aid to inland navigation and has become one of Mount Dora's best-known landmarks and photo opportunities. The lighthouse was dedicated in 1988 and is built of stucco-covered brick. Its light guides boaters on Lake Dora safely to the adjacent boat ramps and Mount Dora Boating Center & Marina.

169 PENSACOLA LIGHTHOUSE

2081 Radford Boulevard
Pensacola, FL 32508; 850-393-1561
pensacolalighthouse.org

The Pensacola Lighthouse and Maritime Museum is located on Naval Air Station Pensacola, adjacent to the National Naval Aviation Museum. The tower was built in 1859 and has a spectacular view of the Gulf Coast. You can climb up the 177 steps to the top, where the view includes Pensacola Pass, Pensacola Bay, three historic forts, the downtown skyline of Pensacola, and the historic Navy Yard. You can also make a reservation to have front-row seats for a Blue Angels practice. The lighthouse and museum are open to the public daily. All civilian visitors must enter through the Public Gate, located just south of the intersection of Blue Angel Parkway and Gulf Beach Highway, and must present proper photo identification (see website for details).

170 PONCE DE LEON INLET LIGHTHOUSE

4931 South Peninsula Drive
Ponce Inlet, FL 32127; 386-761-1821
ponceinlet.org

Designated a National Historic Landmark, Ponce de Leon Inlet Lighthouse is on the inlet that connects the Halifax River to the Atlantic Ocean, about 12 miles south of Daytona Beach. It is not only Florida's tallest lighthouse but also the second-tallest masonry lighthouse in the country, behind only the Hatteras Lighthouse on the Outer Banks of North Carolina. The structure is 175 feet high and takes 203 steps to climb. Self-guided tour maps are provided, or you can take a guided tour. The view from the top is worth the climb: You will see the high-rise condos and beaches to the north in Daytona Beach and to the south in New Smyrna Beach. The museum has interesting displays of various lights that have been in operation at the lighthouse and of the living quarters of the keepers who served there. The lighthouse and museum are open to the public daily except for Thanksgiving and Christmas.

171 PORT BOCA GRANDE LIGHTHOUSE AND MUSEUM

880 Belcher Road
Boca Grande, FL 33921; 941-964-0060
floridastateparks.org/parks-and-trails/gasparilla-island-state-park bips.org/port-boca-grande-lighthouse

The Port Boca Grande Lighthouse and Museum is located on the south end of Gasparilla Island at Gasparilla Island State Park. The lighthouse was built in 1890 and has been restored nearly to its original condition. It is the oldest structure on Gasparilla Island. The lighthouse museum covers the cultural history of the area from 12,000 B.C. to the present time. One of the museum rooms is a "please touch" area where you can examine local bones, fossils, and shells. The museum also has a gift shop. One of the nicest things about this lighthouse is the porch, where you can sit on the gliders and enjoy the beach and the sounds of the sea. The state park is open daily from 8 a.m. to sunset. The hours of operation of the lighthouse and museum vary seasonally.

172 ST. AUGUSTINE LIGHTHOUSE

100 Red Cox Road
St. Augustine, FL 32080
904-829-0745
staugustinelighthouse.org

St. Augustine Lighthouse is on Anastasia Island between downtown St. Augustine and the Atlantic Ocean. Built in 1871–74 on the site of an old Spanish watchtower dating back to the 1500s, the lighthouse is 165 feet above sea level. From the top viewing platform—219 steps up—you see a breathtaking view of St. Augustine, the ocean, the beach, and Salt Run with its boat anchorage. The light is still operational and is a pleasant addition to the St. Augustine skyline. The facilities are operated by the St. Augustine Lighthouse and Maritime Museum, which provides a wide variety of educational programs for schoolchildren and coordinates the visits of the many tourists who come each year.

173 ST. MARKS LIGHTHOUSE

1255 Lighthouse Road
St. Marks, FL 32327; 850-925-6121
stmarksrefuge.org/

This lighthouse is in the St. Marks National Wildlife Refuge about 25 miles south of Tallahassee. It is the second-oldest lighthouse in Florida and the oldest on Florida's Gulf Coast. The current tower was built in 1842. The nearby town of St. Marks was an important port of entry in the early days of American-owned Florida. This lighthouse was built to facilitate entry to the port. The tower and keeper's house were recently restored, and the keeper's quarters are open for tours Friday–Sunday, 11 a.m. to 3 p.m.; however, visitors may not climb the tower.

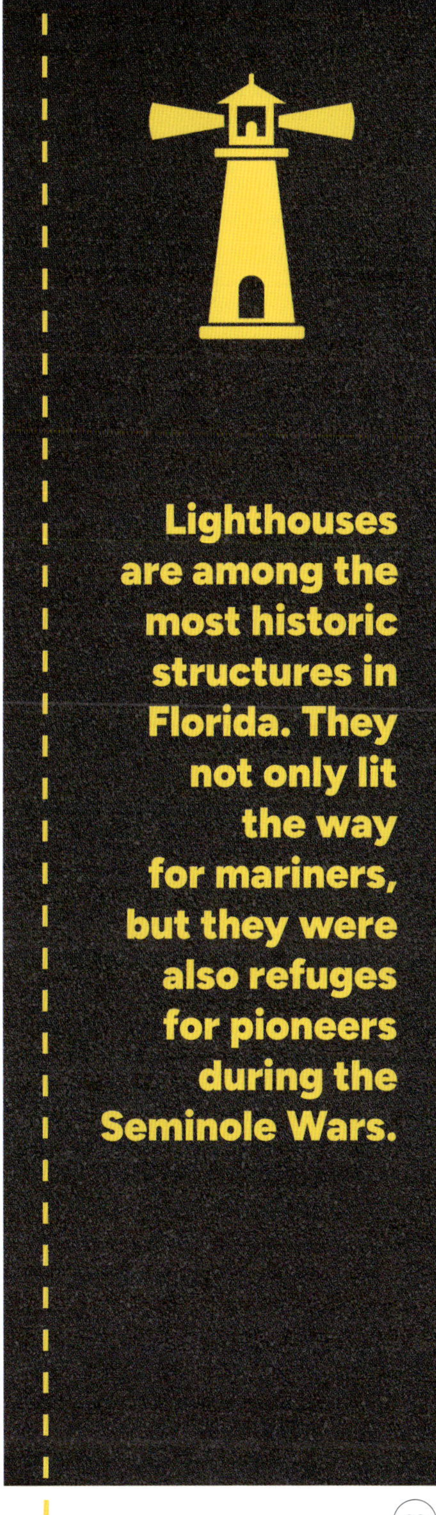

THE LIGHTNER MUSEUM, ST. AUGUSTINE

There are museums in Florida for just about any interest you might have.

From fine Tiffany art to the bizarre collections in a Ripley's Believe it or Not! museum, you name it, and it is probably available for viewing somewhere in the state. Museums range from the serious, such as the state museums of history and natural history, to sports-themed and automobile-oriented museums, and they contain some of the most interesting artifacts in Florida, such as treasure recovered from Spanish shipwrecks.

Welcome to MUSEUMS

Dr. John Gorrie is considered by many to be the inventor of air-conditioning and refrigeration. You can visit a museum in Apalachicola dedicated to his work.

1 OF 5 FACTORY PRODUCED GRAN SPORT CORVETTES PRODUCED IN 1962 AND 1963. THE FOURTH MEMBER SHOWN HERE IS OWNED BY THE REVS INSTITUTE, NAPLES

Find out more about MUSEUMS

174 ALBIN POLASEK MUSEUM & SCULPTURE GARDENS

633 Osceola Avenue
Winter Park, FL 32789; 407-647-6294
polasek.org

Albin Polasek (1879–1965) was one of America's foremost sculptors. He retired to Winter Park in 1950 and designed his home to have a functioning sculpture studio. A few months after retirement, he suffered a stroke and used a wheelchair for the remainder of his life, yet he was still able to complete 18 major works here before he died. In 1961, his home and gallery were first opened to the public. The sculpture gardens are colorful and lush, with many native Floridian and subtropical plants.

175 CHARLES HOSMER MORSE MUSEUM OF AMERICAN ART

445 North Park Avenue
Winter Park, FL 32789; 407-645-5311
morsemuseum.org

With more than 19,000 square feet of public exhibition space, the Morse Museum is home to the world's most comprehensive collection of works by Louis Comfort Tiffany (1848–1933), including not only jewelry and leaded-glass lamps and windows but also pottery, paintings, and art glass. The chapel interior he designed for the 1893 World's Columbian Exposition in Chicago was installed in 1999, four years after the museum's opening. The holdings also include art and architectural elements from Tiffany's Long Island country estate, along with works by his contemporaries, with a particular focus on the Arts and Crafts style.

176 DON GARLITS MUSEUM OF DRAG RACING

13700 SW 16th Avenue
Ocala, FL 34473; 352-245-8661
garlits.com

"Big Daddy" Don Garlits is a legend in the world of drag racing. His series of 34 hand-built race cars propelled him to wins in 144 national events. The Garlits museum has 90 race cars on display in the Drag Race building, as well as 50 other cars in the Antique Car collection. The museum is also home to the International Drag Racing Hall of Fame and includes cars and memorabilia from other famous names in the sport of drag racing. Call a few days in advance to arrange a private, behind-the-scenes tour with "Big Daddy" himself.

177 EDISON AND FORD WINTER ESTATES

2350 McGregor Boulevard
Fort Myers, FL 33901; 239-334-7419
edisonfordwinterestates.org

See inside the side-by-side homes of Thomas Edison and Henry Ford on the Caloosahatchee River in Fort Myers. The combined property also includes Edison's 20 acres of gardens; his botanical research laboratory; and the 15,000-square-foot Edison Ford Museum, which contains inventions, artifacts, and Edison's Model T (a gift from Ford). There are also many displays outlining the biographies of the two men. The entire site is a Florida Historic Landmark and hosts many events, including weddings, corporate meetings, and educational programs.

178 FLORIDA MUSEUM OF NATURAL HISTORY

University of Florida Cultural Plaza
3215 Hull Road
Gainesville, FL 32611; 352-846-2000
floridamuseum.ufl.edu

This museum on the campus of the University of Florida is the official natural history museum of the state. The permanent exhibits focus on the flora, fauna, fossils, and historical people of Florida. An example of the size of this museum is the McGuire Center, which contains 10 million specimens of butterflies and moths. The Mammalogy Collection has more than 38,000 specimens, and the Ichthyology Collection holds roughly 2.5 million fish specimens. Admission is free (though there is a cover charge for featured exhibits and the Butterfly Rainforest), and one could easily spend a week or even a month and not be able to see everything.

179 JACKSONVILLE MUSEUM OF SCIENCE & HISTORY

1025 Museum Circle
Jacksonville, FL 32207; 904-396-6674
themosh.org

Known locally as MOSH, this is Jacksonville's most-visited museum, specializing in science and local history. The main exhibit changes quarterly, and the museum is also home to the Bryan-Gooding Planetarium. Interactive exhibits help you learn about your own body's systems. There are also interactive energy exhibits and several animal encounters. An unusual feature of this museum is its science-and-history boat tours on the adjacent St. Johns River.

180 JOHN GORRIE MUSEUM STATE PARK

46 Sixth Street
Apalachicola, FL 32320; 850-653-9347
floridastateparks.org/parks-and-trails/john-gorrie-museum-state-park

This state park's main exhibits feature the history of the Apalachicola area and focus specifically on the life and inventions of John Gorrie. This museum should actually be a shrine worshipped by all Floridians, as Dr. Gorrie was a pioneer in the development of air-conditioning. A physician, a scientist, an inventor, and a humanitarian, he received the first US patent for mechanical refrigeration in 1851. His ice-making machine was the result of his search for a way to cool his patients' rooms.

181 THE LIGHTNER MUSEUM

75 King Street
St. Augustine, FL 32084
904-824-2874
lightnermuseum.org

The Lightner Museum is in the former Alcazar Hotel, which was built in 1888. It has a large collection of fine and decorative 19th-century art, much of it from the Gilded Age. The first floor houses a Victorian village with shop fronts representing period stores selling period goods. There are examples of cut glass, stained glass, and period furniture pieces. There is even a small mummy, a model steam engine, a player piano, and a golden elephant carrying the Earth on its back.

182 MCLARTY TREASURE MUSEUM

Sebastian Inlet State Park
13180 North FL A1A
Vero Beach, FL 32963; 772-589-2147
floridastateparks.org/parks-and-trails/sebastian-inlet-state-park

The small McLarty Treasure Museum, part of Sebastian Inlet State Park, takes you back to the days when the Spanish treasure fleets voyaged from the Caribbean to Spain more than 300 years ago. Eleven ships were lost in a hurricane in 1715, and salvagers are still working to recover gold, silver, and jewels that were lost from the fleet. The museum features artifacts, displays, and an observation deck that overlooks the Atlantic Ocean.

183 MUSEUM OF FLORIDA HISTORY

500 South Bronough Street
Tallahassee, FL 32399; 850-245-6400
museumoffloridahistory.com

This is the official history museum of the state of Florida, highlighting artifacts and eras unique to Florida and the roles Floridians have played nationally and globally. Exhibits change frequently and have featured Floridian artists, quintessential Floridian imagery, posters from films made in the state, Seminole history, and more. The museum also operates The Knott House Museum, where the Emancipation Proclamation was read in 1865, declaring freedom for all enslaved people in greater Tallahassee.

CALUSA PEOPLE EXHIBIT AT THE FLORIDA MUSEUM OF NATURAL HISTORY, GAINESVILLE

184 NATIONAL NAVY UDT-SEAL MUSEUM

3300 North FL A1A
North Hutchinson Island
Fort Pierce, FL 34949; 772-595-5845
navysealmuseum.org

The National Navy UDT-SEAL Museum has an unusual collection of artifacts and exhibits dedicated to the famous warriors of the US Navy SEAL teams and their predecessors, the Underwater Demolition Teams (UDT). Exhibits include a special-operations boat; a Black Hawk helicopter; weaponry; and even a display about Barry, a canine who bears the title of Naval Special Warfare Group Two's "first dog," who served in over 225 combat missions.

185 ORANGE COUNTY REGIONAL HISTORY CENTER

65 East Central Boulevard
Orlando, FL 32801; 407-836-8500
thehistorycenter.org

This museum in downtown Orlando focuses on the history of central Florida. Among the exhibits are those chronicling African American history, aviation history, and the cattle and citrus industries. Also featured are the history of Florida tourism, the Spanish era, and the Indigenous tribes who lived in Florida before the arrival of the Europeans in the 1500s. The region's flora, fauna, and geography are explained, as is the area's transformation by theme parks. A furnished 19th-century pioneer cabin is also on display here.

186 THE REVS INSTITUTE

2500 South Horseshoe Drive
Naples, FL 34104; 239-687-7387
revsinstitute.org

This museum was only recently opened to the public. It houses the formerly private Miles Collier Collection, one of the world's premier automobile collections, containing more than 100 beautiful automobiles manufactured between 1896 and 1995. Each car in the collection is rare and historically significant, the flagship vehicle being the 1939 Mercedes W154 Grand Prix (the "Silver Arrow").

187 RIPLEY'S BELIEVE IT OR NOT! MUSEUM

19 San Marco Avenue
St. Augustine, FL 32084
904-824-1606
ripleys.com/staugustine

This is a museum you must see to believe. Housed in an 1887 castle-like building, it specializes in bizarre events and objects that are so strange they defy belief, including real shrunken heads, a three-story Erector Set Ferris wheel, and a wax replica of the world's tallest man. Opened in 1950 as the first permanent Ripley's Believe It or Not! Museum, it is now one of 30 Ripley's "odditoriums," but I like this one the most.

RIPLEY'S BELIEVE IT OR NOT! MUSEUM, ST. AUGUSTINE

HIKING WITHLACOOCHEE STATE TRAIL, FLORAL CITY

Florida's year-round temperate-to-tropical climate makes it a perfect place for outdoor adventure.

The state is bordered by roughly 8,400 miles of saltwater coast, and its interior is bejeweled by more than 7,000 lakes and ponds and thousands of miles of rivers and streams. Florida has an extensive state park system, along with national parks, local parks, and bike trails. There are limitless places for boating, fishing, or just plain beachcombing and shell hunting. Florida is made for enjoying the outdoors.

Welcome to OUTDOOR ADVENTURES

Find out more about OUTDOOR ADVENTURES

188 AMELIA ISLAND HORSEBACK RIDING

4600 Peters Point Road
Amelia Island, FL 32034; 904-753-1701
ameliaislandhorsebackriding.com

If you've ever dreamed of galloping through foamy surf on a fast horse, this adventure is for you. Robin A. owns and operates this unique service, which was established in 1993 by Debbie Manser. You call (or book online) and arrange to meet at Peters Point Beachfront Park in Fernandina Beach, and Robin trailers the horses in from stables close to Amelia Island. Once you start riding on the beach, you will do so for 1 hour. Robin can accommodate two to four riders at a time and, with advance notice, can handle up to six.

189 BABCOCK RANCH ECO-TOURS

8502 FL 31
Punta Gorda, FL 33982; 800-500-5583
babcockranchecotours.com

Dating back to the 1800s, Babcock is among the oldest ranches in Florida's long history of cattle ranching. Encompassing a working cattle ranch with over 55,000 acres of pastureland, it is typical of what Old Florida was all about. On their 90-minute Swamp Buggy Eco-Tour, you will traverse Floridian ecosystems, seeing the tough bulls and cows known as Florida Cracker cattle, which are unique to the state, and possibly catching a glimpse of an endangered Florida panther in its wild home. You will also be next to the new solar-powered community of Babcock Ranch, a large planned development on part of the ranch.

190 GINNIE SPRINGS OUTDOORS

5000 NE 60th Avenue
High Springs, FL 32643; 386-454-7188
ginniespringsoutdoors.com

Ginnie Springs Outdoors is a privately owned park that offers a variety of outdoor activities. You can scuba dive, snorkel, camp, go canoeing and kayaking, and enjoy the 200-acre, natural Floridian setting. There are 129 full-service campsites on the property, along with picnic tables, grills, and bathrooms to serve the campsites. The water in the springs is crystal clear and even received praise from Jacques Cousteau, the father of scuba diving.

191 GOLFING

Statewide
pga.com/golf-courses/details/fl

With its year-round temperate climate, Florida is a golfer's paradise. There are courses ranging from small public facilities to tournament-quality private clubs. No matter where in Florida's 67 counties you find yourself, there is sure to be a golf course nearby.

192 ICHETUCKNEE INNER TUBE TRIP

Ichetucknee Springs State Park
12087 SW US 27
Fort White, FL 32038; 386-497-4690
floridastateparks.org/park/ichetucknee-springs

Floating down the Ichetucknee River is a Floridian tradition that spans many generations. The crystal-clear river flows 6 miles through shady natural hillocks and wetlands before it reaches the Santa Fe River. There are several private concessions, in addition to the public state park, where inner tubes can be rented. The tubing season lasts from Memorial Day weekend to Labor Day weekend.

193 KAYAKING AT TOPSAIL HILL PRESERVE STATE PARK

7525 West County Highway 30A
Santa Rosa Beach, FL 32459
850-267-8330
floridastateparks.org/park/topsail-hill

Topsail Hill is one of Florida's natural treasures. It includes miles of white-sand beaches along the Gulf Coast, with dunes more than 25 feet high. It also features three rare coastal dune lakes. Visitors can canoe, kayak, or paddleboard on the Gulf. Personal watercraft can be rented at the park.

194 SCALLOPING IN THE GULF

Florida Fish and Wildlife Conservation Commission
620 South Meridian Street
Tallahassee, FL 32399; 850-488-4676
myfwc.com/fishing/saltwater/recreational/bay-scallops

Scalloping season is usually July to September. During season, thousands of people gather along the Gulf Coast from south of Steinhatchee up to the Carrabelle area. Their fishing equipment consists of snorkel gear and buckets. A saltwater fishing license is required to harvest the tasty little critters, unless you wade into the shallow waters and feel for the animals with your feet and hands without using a mask or snorkel.

195 SEA TURTLES NESTING

Sea Turtle Preservation Society
111 South Miramar Avenue
Indialantic, FL 32903; 321-676-1701
seaturtlespacecoast.org

Florida has an abundant supply of beautiful sand beaches, and sea turtle nesting season runs every year from May to October. The mother turtles crawl up the beach to the dune line, dig holes in the sand, and lay their eggs. Some experts say that sea turtles make 40,000–84,000 nests each year on Florida beaches. A favorite place to observe this nesting activity is on Florida's east coast. The Sea Turtle Preservation Society is located near the center of this stretch, in Indialantic near Melbourne Beach. When observing sea turtles, never disturb a nest or use flash photography or shine lights on nests.

BABY SEA TURTLE HATCHLING CRAWLING TOWARD THE OCEAN

196 TROY SPRINGS STATE PARK

674 NE Troy Springs Road
Branford, FL 32008; 386-935-4835
floridastateparks.org/learn/swimming-and-diving-troy-spring

A diver's paradise, this park features a 70-foot-deep spring along the Suwannee River. It's popular for scuba diving (especially for training), swimming, and snorkeling, with the remains of a Civil War–era steamboat visible underwater. It's a peaceful spot with picnic areas and trails too.

A DIVER ENTERING THE SPRING WATERS OF TROY SPRINGS STATE PARK, BRANFORD

197 WITHLACOOCHEE STATE TRAIL

3100 South Old Floral City Road
Inverness, FL 34450; 352-726-0315
floridastateparks.org/trail/withlacoochee

The Withlacoochee State Trail is a 46-mile-long path that follows an abandoned railroad route that ran roughly parallel to the nearby Withlacoochee River. The path is now paved and is a great location to hike, bike (no motors), and skate. It's mostly flat, so it's a relatively easy and enjoyable outing. You can start the path at either end (north or south) or at one of the towns or villages along the route. There are stores along the trail and restrooms too. There is also a bike repair-and-rental shop in Floral City.

198 ZIP LINES

Statewide
ziplinerider.com/Florida_Ziplines.html

Zip-lining is another year-round outdoor activity made possible by Florida's moderate climate. Zip lines are found in many adventure courses and theme parks, and in Florida a large number of them are located in natural settings where you can soar through the treetops. There are even places where you can fly safely above alligators and other wildlife. Some of the zip lines are for beginners, and others involve challenging obstacle courses.

IT'S A LONG WAY DOWN!

DRY TORTUGAS NATIONAL PARK, KEY WEST

Parks in Florida are treasured natural resources.

The Old Florida that is rapidly disappearing is being preserved in local, state, and national parks. It is because of these parks that some parts of natural Florida are still alive and well despite the proliferation of condos, theme parks, subdivisions, and shopping malls, which have obliterated much of the landscape in the past half century or so. Many state parks have campsites carved out of the surrounding piney woods and palmettos. This natural vegetation gives the sites much greater privacy than you might find in the average private campground.

Welcome to

PARKS

Find out more about PARKS

199 BISCAYNE NATIONAL PARK

9700 SW 328th Street
Sir Lancelot Jones Way
Homestead, FL 33033; 305-230-1144
nps.gov/bisc

I have enjoyed sailing in Biscayne Bay more than anywhere else in Florida. Even though it is in the heart of Miami and the rest of urbanized south Florida, it has some of the clearest waters in the state. This is because much of the bay is within Biscayne National Park. The park is nearly 173,000 acres and is 95% underwater. It's a thrill to be boating within sight of the massive skyscrapers of downtown Miami while still feeling worlds away. If you love the outdoors, you will enjoy yourself in this park. You can snorkel, camp, boat, watch wildlife, fish, take guided eco-adventures, or just relax. Several private concessions offer full-day tours in the park that include snorkeling, hiking, paddling, and sailing. Mainland access is from park headquarters at Convoy Point. Local parks and marinas also provide access. The park protects Stiltsville, once a community of 27 houses perched on stilts. Only a few buildings survived Hurricane Andrew in 1992, and they are all unoccupied. The park has a few mooring buoys near Fowey Rocks lighthouse for private boaters. Personal watercraft such as Jet Skis are prohibited.

200 DEVIL'S MILLHOPPER GEOLOGICAL STATE PARK

4732 Millhopper Road
Gainesville, FL 32653;
352-955-2008
floridastateparks.org/parks-and-trails/devils-millhopper-geological-state-park

I have been a resident of the Sunshine State for most of my life, and this park is unlike anywhere else in the rest of Florida. This geological wonder will give you the feeling of being in another world. You walk down a 132-step wooden staircase into the bottom of a geological formation that has been attracting visitors for well over a century: a sinkhole that is 120 feet deep and has a diameter of 500 feet. The geology here has created a miniature rainforest in the middle of north-central Florida. You will see gentle streams of clear water trickling down the limestone walls. These miniature waterfalls, and the natural coolness of the place, make it a refreshing escape from the busy Florida environment that surrounds it. Sometimes volunteer guides are on duty and will happily share inside stories about the park with you. Open daily year-round, there is a minimal entrance fee to visit.

201 DRY TORTUGAS NATIONAL PARK

40001 FL 9336
Homestead, FL 33034; 305-242-7700
nps.gov/drto

You can take a long day trip or enjoy a camping adventure by visiting Dry Tortugas National Park, about 70 miles west of Key West. This 100-square-mile park is made up of seven small islands and is accessible only by boat or seaplane. The park is famous for its centerpiece attraction, the imposing Fort Jefferson, the place where Dr. Mudd was imprisoned for treating John Wilkes Booth's broken leg after President Lincoln's assassination. The islands are surrounded by clear, blue waters; beautiful coral reefs teeming with marine life; and a large bird population. There are several popular ways to make the trip to the park. You can bring your own boat, charter a boat or seaplane in Key West, or take a passenger ferry. The way I prefer is to take the *Yankee Freedom III*, a high-speed catamaran ferry that takes about 2 hours and 10 minutes. It stays at the park for about 4 hours, giving you plenty of time to explore.

202 FLORIDA CAVERNS STATE PARK

3345 Caverns Road
Marianna, FL 32446; 850-482-1228
floridastateparks.org/parks-and-trails/florida-caverns-state-park

This is another natural attraction that will make you feel as though you are not in Florida. It is your chance to explore a network of underground caves created from limestone formations that have slowly dissolved over thousands of years. You will enjoy the cool air, the drip-drip-drip of trickling water, and breathtaking views of mysterious stalactites and stalagmites. You will move from cave to cave and see the many chisel marks made in the 1930s by Civilian Conservation Corps workers, who enlarged the cave passageways by hand so visitors could stand upright during guided tours. These workers also built the park's spacious visitor center. Prior to Hurricane Michael in 2018, the park also offered multi-use trails, camping, boating, and fishing; however, due to damage sustained in the hurricane, only the ranger station, visitor center, museum, and cave tours are currently open. Please check the website for the latest updates.

PANORAMIC VIEW OF A LIT ROOM INSIDE THE CAVE AT FLORIDA CAVERNS STATE PARK, MARIANNA

203 FRUIT & SPICE PARK

24801 SW 187th Avenue
Homestead, FL 33031; 305-247-5727
miamidade.gov/fruitandspicepark/home.page

Fruit & Spice Park is one of the most unusual parks in Florida. It was an eye-opener to me when I realized that fruit and spices could be so much fun. The park is in the heart of an agricultural wonder called the Redland, named for the predominant red clay soil. Plants grow in the Redland that won't grow elsewhere in Florida or America, including species native to tropical areas of Asia or South America. More than 500 varieties of exotic fruits, vegetables, herbs, spices, and nuts from all over the world are found in the 37-acre Fruit & Spice Park, established in 1944 and operated by Miami-Dade County. Its collection includes specimens from the Americas, Africa, Australia and the Pacific, Asia, and the Mediterranean, including many fruit varieties of mangoes, bananas, and jackfruit trees. The park has a nice little café serving salads, sandwiches, wraps, and pizza. The friendly staff will let you sample some of the garden delights from a serving platter they keep on hand. Guided tours of the park are conducted daily at 11 a.m, 1:30 p.m, and 3 p.m.

204 HIGHLANDS HAMMOCK STATE PARK

5931 Hammock Road
Sebring, FL 33872; 863-386-6094
floridastateparks.org/parks-and-trails/highlands-hammock-state-park

I love driving through this beautiful park. If I have more time, I take a tram ride and let somebody else do the driving. You can also hike on its nine trails or ride your bike on a 3-mile-loop trail. Open since 1931, it's one of the oldest state parks and has more than 9,000 acres that encompass a thriving ecosystem. Highlands Hammock has one of Florida's most diverse collections of plant and animal life, with 1,000-year-old oaks, old-growth hillock, and Florida panthers. Ferns and air plants are almost everywhere you look. You might even see a black bear. An elevated boardwalk crosses a cypress swamp, and from there you may see alligators, birds, and other wildlife. Picnicking, birdwatching, and ranger-guided tours are other popular activities. The tram tour gives you the opportunity to view wildlife relatively close-up, in areas of the park that are restricted to public access. Highlands Hammock also provides a full-facility campground.

VISITORS TO HIGHLANDS HAMMOCK STATE PARK STROLL ON A WOODEN WALKWAY, SEBRING

205 MARJORIE KINNAN RAWLINGS HISTORIC STATE PARK

18700 South County Road 325
Cross Creek, FL 32640; 352-466-3672
floridastateparks.org/parks-and-trails/marjorie-kinnan-rawlings-historic-state-park

Marjorie Kinnan Rawlings won the Pulitzer Prize for her novel *The Yearling*. She also wrote a book titled *Cross Creek* about her years living here. She wrote both books here in her little house, and you will see her old typewriter and feel as though she might pop back into the room at any minute. Her Florida Cracker–style home and farm have been preserved and restored, allowing visitors to experience what 1930s farm life was like when she lived and worked here. The park is open daily, and rangers in period costume lead tours of the house October–July, Thursday–Sunday at 10 and 11 a.m. and at 1, 2, and 3 p.m. You can also explore Rawlings's farmyard, grove, seasonal garden, and trails. A nearby park has a picnic area, a boat ramp, and a playground.

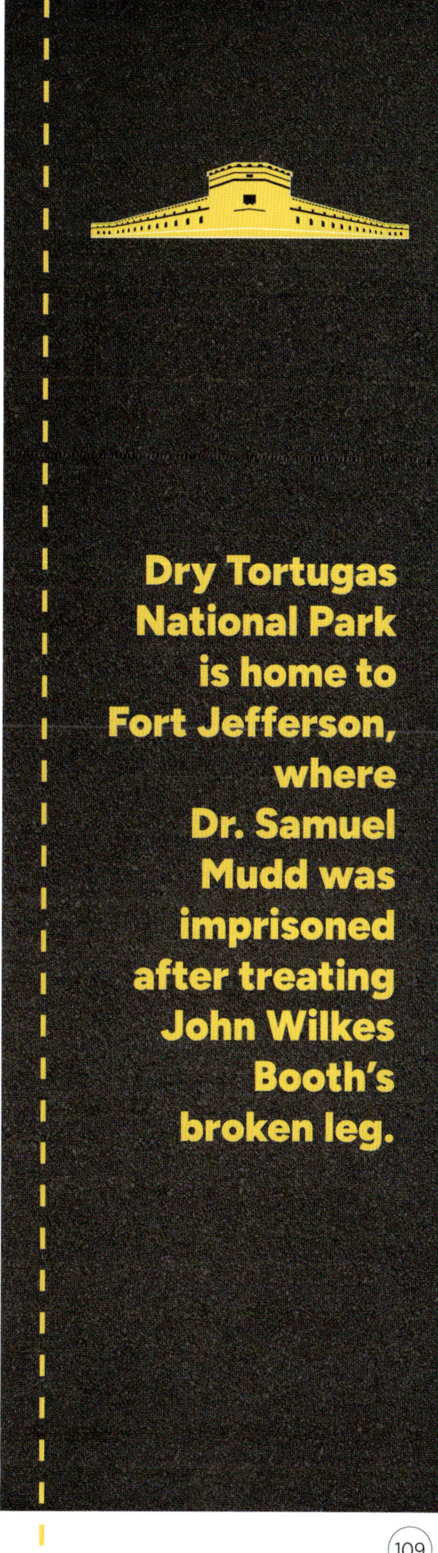

SATURN V ROCKET ON DISPLAY

Florida's modern history began first with railroads, then airplanes, and finally rockets.

After the Civil War, water routes were the main method of transportation in the state. Railroads made the development of Florida possible by increasing export routes for its agricultural products and enabling tourists to come down from the North. Aviation followed during World Wars I and II, and the modern space program began in Florida at Cape Canaveral with the launch of *Bumper 8* in 1950. Federal, state, and local governments, along with private individuals, have done a great job preserving the memories and artifacts of these eras.

Welcome to
ROCKETS, AIRPLANES & RAILROADS

Find out more about

ROCKETS, AIRPLANES & RAILROADS

206 AEROSPACE DISCOVERY AT THE FLORIDA AIR MUSEUM

4075 James C. Ray Drive
Lakeland, FL 33811; 863-644-2431
flysnf.org

Designated as Florida's "Official Aviation Museum and Education Center," this museum is housed in a building on the campus of the Sun 'n Fun Aerospace Expo at Lakeland Linder International Airport. The museum features a display of one-of-a-kind designs, classics, ultralights, antiques, and war planes. In addition to aircraft, there is a large collection of aircraft engines from World War I to the present day. Aerospace Discovery at the Florida Air Museum continues to grow and is becoming a showcase for Florida's aviation history through exhibits, restoration and preservation, education, and outreach so that all ages may share the "passion for flight."

207 AIR FORCE ARMAMENT MUSEUM

100 Museum Drive
Eglin Air Force Base, FL 32542
850-882-4062
afarmamentmuseum.com

The museum showcases the armament of aviation warfare from World War II all the way to today's high-technology planes, guns, and bombs. It has a large collection of weapons and cockpit simulators that will keep an aviation buff busy for hours. As you drive onto the museum property, you will see many aircraft on display, including the SR-71 Blackbird, the fastest crewed, air-breathing plane ever built. There are other planes from World War II, the Korean War, the Vietnam War, and the Persian Gulf War. There are four more aircraft inside the museum building itself, as well as a huge variety of bombs, missiles, and rockets.

AN A-10 THUNDERBOLT II AT THE AIR FORCE ARMAMENT MUSEUM, EGLIN AIR FORCE BASE

208 CAPE CANAVERAL SPACE FORCE MUSEUM

Launch Complex 26
Cape Canaveral Space Force Station, FL 32925; 321-853-9171
ccspacemuseum.org

The museum includes many exhibits about the history of rocketry and space flight, and the grounds encompass two adjoining launch complexes: 26 and 5/6. Launch Complex 26 is the site of the first successful launch of an American satellite, *Explorer I,* in 1958. From 1957 until its deactivation in 1963, Launch Complex 26 conducted 36 launches. These launches included the three monkeys that led the way for crewed space flights. Launch Complex 5/6 was the launch site for the earliest Project Mercury missions. It was from Pad 5 in 1961 that Alan Shepard and Gus Grissom were launched into space. You can schedule tours online.

209 CENTRAL FLORIDA RAILROAD MUSEUM

101 South Boyd Street
Winter Garden, FL 34787
407-656-0559
cfrhs.org

This small museum is managed by the Central Florida Chapter of the National Railway Historical Society and focuses on the railroads of central Florida. Among items exhibited are historical photographs, including an extensive collection of Tavares & Gulf Railroad photographs from its early steam era until its last run. You will also see lanterns, locks, old telephones, telegraphs, signs, stoves, tools, furniture, timetables, dining-car tableware, ticket punches, lamps, uniforms, locomotive bells and whistles, a 1938 Fairmont motorcar, and a velocipede hand car. A caboose is on display outside the museum, along with a three-head interlocking signal from a former junction in Plant City, a set of narrow-gauge wheels, and several switch stands and crossing signals.

210 FANTASY OF FLIGHT

1400 Broadway Boulevard SE
Polk City, FL 33868; 863-984-3500
fantasyofflight.com

You will be amazed at what you see and experience here. Aviation pioneer Kermit Weeks opened Fantasy of Flight in 1995 to share his love for aviation and aircraft. It is home to the world's largest private collection of vintage aircraft. There are more than 140 civilian and military planes, and many are air-worthy. A portion of the collection is always on display. There are also themed immersion experiences, flight simulators, interactive exhibits, and tram tours. It is a great place to learn about aviation history. One good way to see the place is by taking a guided tour. It is also useful to check out Fantasy of Flight's Facebook page and that of Kermit Weeks to see what is currently happening. Fantasy of Flight even has its own airfield, shown on the charts as "Orlampa," so named because it is about halfway between Orlando and Tampa.

211 FLORIDA RAILROAD MUSEUM

12210 83rd Street East
Parrish, FL 34219; 941-776-0906
frrm.org

It you love trains, there is a lot to love here. This is one of three official state railroad museums in Florida. The museum has a large collection of rolling stock, including 13 locomotives; 9 passenger cars, including Pullmans; 6

cabooses; and various kinds of freight cars. Some of the locomotives and cars are in service, and the others are for display only. The ticket office and gift shop are open Wednesday–Sunday, and 13-mile train rides take place on most Saturdays and Sundays, departing at 11 a.m. and 2 p.m. The locomotive pulls cars consisting of open-window coaches, a covered gondola, and an air-conditioned coach.

212 KENNEDY SPACE CENTER VISITOR COMPLEX

Space Commerce Way
Merritt Island, FL 32953
855-433-4210
kennedyspacecenter.com

Kennedy Space Center is where the United States began its journey into space and where that journey continues to this day. There is so much to see and do here that at least one day should be set aside to make your visit worthwhile. The website lets you plan your trip in advance and choose your own itinerary based on the age of any children in your party and how many days you have to spend. The complex features exhibits and displays, historic spacecraft and memorabilia, shows, an IMAX theater, and a range of bus tours of the spaceport. *The Space Shuttle Atlantis* exhibit is home to the orbiter of the same name, and the Shuttle Launch Experience is a simulated trip into space. The complex also has daily presentations from a veteran NASA astronaut. A bus tour, included with admission, encompasses the separate Apollo/Saturn V Center. You will be among the approximately 1.5 million annual visitors who enjoy the complex.

213 MURDER MYSTERY DINNER TRAIN

Colonial Station
2805 Colonial Boulevard
Fort Myers, FL 33966; 239-275-8487
semgulf.com

Have you ever wanted to go to a murder mystery dinner? Have you ever wanted to ride on a train? Here is your chance to do both! Enjoy a five-course dinner while watching a mystery play—usually a comedy—and helping to solve the murder. You will be given clue sheets before the play and will write down clues as you discover them. Your clue sheet is collected before the final act, when the killer is revealed. Maybe you will win the Super Sleuth award. The train leaves from Fort Myers every Wednesday, Thursday, Friday, Saturday, and Sunday and makes a 40-mile, 3.5-hour round trip. All trains depart promptly at 6:30 p.m. (5:30 p.m. on Sundays).

214 NATIONAL NAVAL AVIATION MUSEUM

1750 Radford Boulevard
Naval Air Station Pensacola, FL 32507
850-452-8450
navalaviationmuseum.org

U.S. Navy pilots are among the best aviators in the world, and their history is celebrated in this fantastic museum at Naval Air Station Pensacola. You will see more than 150 wonderfully restored airplanes and 4,000 other items related to aviation in the Navy, Marines, and Coast Guard. You can sit in a flight simulator to get a feel for what it's like to fly a naval aircraft, and you can also enjoy action-packed movies in the Giant Screen theater. The Flight Deck store has all kinds of souvenirs and mementos related to naval aviation, and there is also a nice café. All visitors to the National Naval Aviation Museum who do not possess a Department of Defense identification card or are not escorted by the holder of a such a card are required to enter and exit Naval Air Station Pensacola through the West Gate at 1878 S. Blue Angel Parkway.

215 VALIANT AIR COMMAND WARBIRD AIR MUSEUM

Space Coast Regional Airport
6600 Tico Road
Titusville, FL 32780; 321-268-1941
valiantaircommand.com

This museum focuses on war planes from the earliest days of aviation to the present day. Its collection includes nearly 50 historic warbirds. At least nine of these planes are privately owned and in flying condition, and their owners permit the planes to be in the collection. Among these is a replica of a Sopwith F.1 Camel, a De Havilland DH.82 Tigermoth, and a TBM Avenger torpedo bomber. The static collection includes about 40 planes, including a Me-208, a MiG-15, and an F-8K Crusader. There is also a memorabilia room with flight gear, dress uniforms, weapons, and other artifacts.

Florida's transportation network started with rivers and Indigenous trails; then came the railroads, automobiles, airplanes, and now space travel.

BLOWING ROCKS PRESERVE, JUPITER ISLAND

The vast biodiversity in Florida makes it an excellent place to study nature.

The rapid development of Florida has been a double-edged sword. On the negative side, this growth has too often been rampant and careless and has done a lot of environmental damage. Some native habitats have been lost forever. On a positive note, the financial resources generated by this growth have provided the funds for organizations to buy sensitive lands for preservation. These preserves, along with nature centers and science museums, continue to educate the public about environmental issues and help them become good stewards of the land.

Welcome to

SCIENCE MUSEUMS & NATURE CENTERS

216 BLOWING ROCKS PRESERVE

574 South Beach Road
Hobe Sound, FL 33455; 561-744-6668
tinyurl.com/blowingrocksfl

You will witness magnificent breaking waves and endangered wildlife at this environmental preserve on Jupiter Island. The limestone outcroppings here are unusual in that they are the largest outcroppings of Anastasia limestone on the East Coast. When the surf is heavy, the waves force themselves through holes in the limestone and can blow ocean spray as high as 50 feet in the air. The barrier island sanctuary harbors manatees and rare loggerhead, green, and leatherback sea turtles, as well as tree species like the sea grape, gumbo-limbo, and mangrove.

217 CORKSCREW SWAMP SANCTUARY

375 Sanctuary Road West
Naples, FL 34120; 239-348-9151
corkscrew.audubon.org

Bring your binoculars when you visit Corkscrew Swamp. In the early days of Florida's development, cypress trees were abundant in the swamps of Florida, but extensive logging operations destroyed most of them by the mid-20th century. This sanctuary has preserved the largest stands of the endangered virgin bald cypress in North America. Stroll along a 2.25-mile boardwalk through pine flatwoods, wet prairies, and stands of bald cypress and learn about the wetland ecosystems. The sanctuary is a major stop on the Great Florida Birding & Wildlife Trail. The endangered wood stork and many other wetland birds breed here. Among species you might see are night herons, tricolored herons, snowy egrets, limpkins, barred owls, and swallow-tailed kites. You may also see otters, deer, turtles, and snakes. You can take a self-guided tour or enjoy one of many guided tours offered by the sanctuary staff.

218 FLORIDA KEYS ECO-DISCOVERY CENTER

35 East Quay Road
Key West, FL 33040; 305-809-4750
floridakeys.noaa.gov/eco_discovery.html

The casual environment of this small, free nature center is just right for laid-back Key West. The center teaches you about the native plants, animals, and ecosystems of the Florida Keys. There are several exhibits, including an interactive satellite map of the Florida Keys. There is also a replica of the Aquarius Reef Base underwater ocean laboratory near Key Largo and an underwater video camera that is used to monitor the health of coral reefs. The Mote Marine Laboratory Living Reef exhibit contains a 2,500-gallon saltwater tank inhabited by tropical fish and living coral.

219 GUMBO LIMBO NATURE CENTER

1801 North Ocean Boulevard
Boca Raton, FL 33432; 561-544-8605
myboca.us/2485/Gumbo-Limbo-Nature-Center

This nature center packs a lot of interesting exhibits into its 20 acres of protected barrier island. Although it has no direct Atlantic Ocean beachfront, it has a shoreline along the Intracoastal Waterway. Its name comes from the gumbo-limbo tree, of which there are many in this park. There are also many other trees, such as the strangler fig and cabbage palm. The center has an indoor museum with exhibits and aquariums, plus several outdoor aquariums displaying ecosystems for fish, turtles, and sea life. You can enjoy a boardwalk trail and experience a small butterfly garden and a Seminole Chiki hut. Gumbo Limbo is well-known for its sea turtle rehabilitation facility, and you can see some of the turtles under its care.

TURTLE AT GUMBO LIMBO NATURE CENTER, BOCA RATON

220 HARBOR BRANCH OCEAN DISCOVERY VISITORS CENTER

5600 North US 1
Fort Pierce, FL 34946; 772-242-2293
fau.edu/hboi/discover-fau-harbor-branch/ocean-discovery-visitors-center

When you step through the doors here, you will be entering Florida Atlantic University's Harbor Branch Oceanographic Institute, a large, functioning research facility with a storied history. Located on a 144-acre site fronting the Indian River Lagoon north of Fort Pierce, its research community includes over 300 ocean scientists, staff, and students. Research is directed toward innovation in marine science and engineering, conservation of coral reefs, the study of marine mammals and fisheries, and more. The visitors center contains a video theater, aquariums, interactive exhibits, and other displays designed to show you the institute's exploration of the marine environment and current research. Exhibits change frequently to reflect ongoing research and conservation efforts. There is no charge for individuals or families.

221 MERRITT ISLAND NATIONAL WILDLIFE REFUGE

1987 Scrub Jay Way
Titusville, FL 32782; 321-861-0669
fws.gov/refuge/merritt_island

It always amazes me to visit this huge refuge, nestled in the shadow of Kennedy Space Center. The space center and the refuge exist side by side on Merritt Island. The unspoiled nature of the refuge and the space-age activity nearby make a dramatic contrast. The refuge is 140,000 acres and boasts over 1,000 species of plants and over 500 species of wildlife. It has miles of public hiking and driving trails. It is also a site on the Great Florida Birding & Wildlife Trail. It's best, but not mandatory, to stop first at the visitor center to get your bearings. A favorite place to see wildlife is the Black Point Wildlife Drive. This is a 7-mile drive along a dirt road through pine flatwoods and marshes. I have made this drive several times and have seen wading birds, alligators, otters, bobcats, snakes, ducks, ospreys, and eagles. You can pick up a brochure near the drive entrance that tells you what to look for. It usually takes a bit less than 1 hour to make this drive.

222 MUSEUM OF SCIENCE & INDUSTRY (MOSI)

4801 East Fowler Avenue
Tampa, FL 33617; 813-987-6000
mosi.org

This museum is fun for people of all ages, with more than 100 hands-on activities. Among its features are a planetarium and several exhibits that explore concepts in science, health and wellness, space, and weather. Build a robot; learn about optical illusions; try to solve hands-on puzzles; explore space in a NASA-funded, simulated lunar colony; and even lie on a bed of nails. Put on a pair of "drunk-driving goggles" to see how alcohol affects your vision and coordination, and learn about 3-D printing and how it is changing the world. Since it's Florida, take the opportunity to experience hurricane-force winds and touch a lightning bolt. At the planetarium, a star projector can simulate the night sky at any place or time on Earth—past, present, or future.

223 OCALA NATIONAL FOREST

Lake George Ranger District
17147 East FL 40
Silver Springs, FL 34488
352-625-2520
fs.usda.gov/ocala

There are many public roads that will take you into north-central Florida's Ocala National Forest. You can wander around wherever you want, but it's more fun to visit their website or stop at a visitor center to get brochures and maps to help plan your visit. The forest covers 387,000 acres and contains much of Florida's remaining sand-pine scrub forest, along with more than 600 lakes, rivers, and springs. The forest is home to black bears, alligators, deer, wild boars, coyotes, foxes, possums, raccoons, otters, bobcats, skunks, armadillos, and gopher tortoises. There are numerous recreation areas, back-road trails, campgrounds, hiking trails, equestrian trails, and scenic byways. The forest also contains four wilderness areas designated by Congress as places that are totally protected from humans. Their ecosystems have completely natural environments and give adventurous people a place to test their wilderness skills, including surviving mosquitoes.

224 ORLANDO SCIENCE CENTER

777 East Princeton Street
Orlando, FL 32803; 407-514-2000
osc.org

With four floors of science exhibits, giant-screen movie theaters, and live programming, this science center offers many interactive experiences in the field of natural science. Get to know a real reptile or learn about the dinosaur age, physics, and gravity. Experience a flight simulator in the Flight Lab, and visit Dr. Dare's Lab to witness experiments in forensics, electricity, or chemistry. On top of the center, the Crosby Observatory has Florida's largest publicly accessible refractor telescope. This 10-inch telescope and several smaller scopes are available at selected times for viewing the sky, weather permitting.

225 WILDLIFE SANCTUARY OF NORTHWEST FLORIDA

105 North South Street
Pensacola, FL 32505; 850-433-9453
pensacolawildlife.com

Each year, this sanctuary provides care to more than 3,000 injured or orphaned wild animals native to Florida. When it receives an animal, staff members provide immediate medical attention and care for the animal until it can be released. Animals they have helped and released include foxes, birds, rabbits, squirrels, possums, raccoons, and skunks. Some animals that cannot be rehabilitated become permanent residents of the sanctuary. It is currently home to more than 50 of these, including bald eagles, hawks, and owls, which you can see on your visit.

Florida has done a good job preserving many natural areas, and its high-tech culture has launched the openings of several modern science museums.

There were many Indigenous tribes living in Florida before the Spanish arrived in the 1500s.

Most of the Indigenous people of Florida disappeared within 200 years, either dying of European diseases or being enslaved in the Caribbean. The Seminoles emerged in the 1700s from a combination of various tribes who settled in Florida. The dominant tribe was the northern Muscogee Creeks from Georgia and Alabama. By 1842, most Seminoles had been forcibly relocated to reservations west of the Mississippi River. The remaining population fought the third of three wars against the United States. In the 20th century, the Miccosukee became its own recognized tribe.

Welcome to SEMINOLE CULTURE

Find out more about

SEMINOLE CULTURE

226 AH-TAH-THI-KI MUSEUM

Big Cypress Seminole Indian Reservation
34725 West Boundary Road
Clewiston, FL 33440; 877-902-1113
ahtahthiki.com

This museum in the heart of the Big Cypress Seminole Indian Reservation has a collection of more than 180,000 artifacts and a variety of on-site artisans. You will learn about the Seminole people and their rich historical and cultural ties to the state of Florida and the southeastern United States. The museum grounds include a 1-mile raised boardwalk that meanders through a 60-acre cypress dome typical of the Everglades. You will also see a Seminole village and ceremonial grounds.

227 BIG CYPRESS RV RESORT

30290 Josie Billie Highway
Clewiston, FL 33440; 800-437-4102
bigcypressrvresort.com

A quieter option on the Big Cypress Reservation, this campground lets visitors stay in Seminole territory. It's near Billie Swamp Safari and the Ah-Tah-Thi-Ki Museum, with RV sites, cabins, and tent camping on the Everglades' edge. Amenities include a pool, places to fish, and proximity to reservation attractions. It's a great base for exploring Seminole culture and nature.

228 DADE BATTLEFIELD HISTORIC STATE PARK

7200 Battlefield Parkway
Bushnell, FL 33513; 352-793-4781
floridastateparks.org/park/dade-battlefield

This park was established in 1921 to preserve and commemorate the site of Dade's Battle of 1835, which precipitated the most devastating of the Seminole Wars. An annual battle reenactment takes place here in January, and a small museum at the visitor center features exhibits such as an award-winning, 12-minute video about the historic battle. The park has beautiful grounds, picnic pavilions, and hiking trails.

229 MICCOSUKEE CASINO & RESORT

500 SW 177th Avenue
Miami, FL 33194; 305-925-2555
miccosukee.com

The Miccosukee tribe was part of the Seminole Nation until the mid-20th century, when they organized as an independent tribe. This resort on the western edge of the Miami metropolitan area is a complete destination featuring modern hotel accommodations, restaurants, gaming, and entertainment venues. While you're there, play a round at one of the Miccosukee Golf & Country Club's three courses, visit an Indian Village, or take an airboat ride. The main Miccosukee reservation is several miles west of the resort on Tamiami Trail (US 41).

230 SEMINOLE HARD ROCK HOTEL & CASINO

1 Seminole Way
Hollywood, FL 33314; 866-502-7529
seminolehardrockhollywood.com

This resort is in urban south Florida and close to beaches and other amenities. It features a large hotel and gaming opportunities, including more than 2,000 slot machines. Entertainment is constantly on offer at the 3,500-seat Hard Rock Event Center. There are several restaurants on the property, including the Hard Rock Cafe. Outdoor activities include a beach club with a pool and bar.

231 SEMINOLE WARS HERITAGE TRAIL

Numerous locations across the state
dos.myflorida.com/historical/preservation/heritage-trails/seminole-wars-heritage-trail

The Seminoles fought three wars against the United States from 1817 to 1858 in a struggle to remain in their ancestral Floridian homeland. The state of Florida offers a free 56-page publication that gives the history of the wars and other Floridian topics. The publication also includes information and locations of battlefields, cemeteries, museum exhibits, monuments, historical markers, and other sites with direct links to the Seminole Wars.

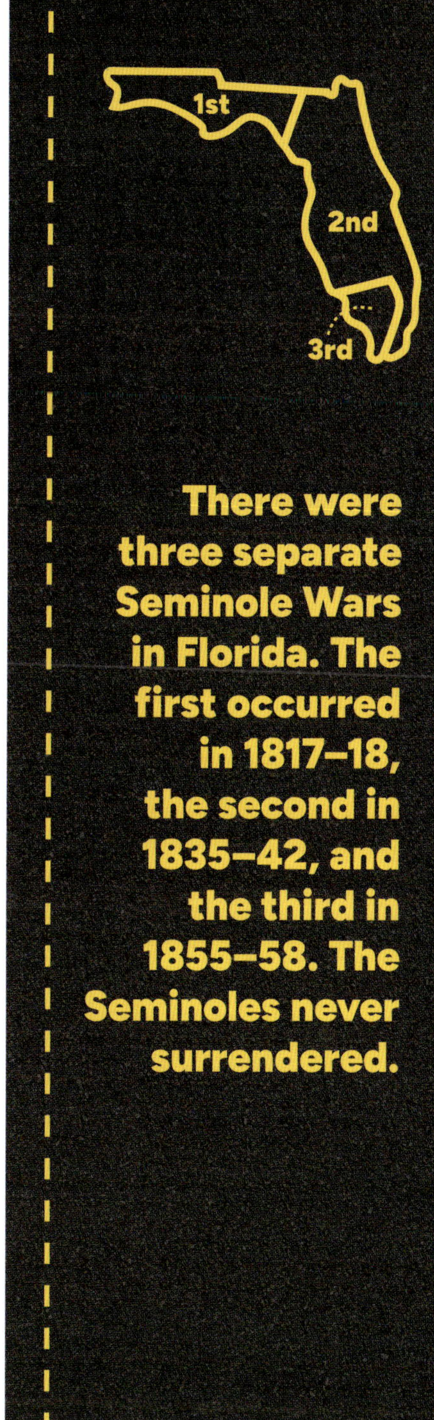

VARIETY OF SPORTS EQUIPMENT

Numerous professional sports teams and several elite college athletic programs call Florida home.

The biggest sport in the state is football, and fans can choose to watch games from the three professional and quite a few college teams. Fans of other sports will be just as happy, though, as the state also has notable basketball, hockey, and soccer teams, to name a few.

Welcome to

SPORTS

232 BASEBALL

232A Miami Marlins
Loan Depot Park
501 Marlins Way
Miami, FL 33125; 305-480-1300
mlb.com/marlins

232B Tampa Bay Rays
Tropicana Field
1 Tropicana Field Drive
St. Petersburg, FL 33705
888-326-7297
mlb.com/rays

233 BASKETBALL

233A Miami Heat
Kaseya Center
601 Biscayne Boulevard
Miami, FL 33132; 786-777-1000
nba.com/heat/home

233B Orlando Magic
Kia Center
400 West Church Street
Orlando, FL 32801; 407-896-2442
nba.com/magic

234 FOOTBALL

234A Jacksonville Jaguars
TIAA Bank Field
1 TIAA Everbank Stadium Drive
Jacksonville, FL 32202; 904-633-2000
jaguars.com

234B Miami Dolphins
Hard Rock Stadium,
347 Don Shula Drive
Miami Gardens, FL 33056
305-943-8000
miamidolphins.com

234C Tampa Bay Buccaneers
Raymond James Stadium
4201 North Dale Mabry Highway
Tampa, FL 33607; 813-870-2700
buccaneers.com

235 HOCKEY

235A Florida Panthers
Amerant Bank Arena
1 Panther Parkway
Sunrise, FL 33323; 954-835-7000
nhl.com/panthers

235B Tampa Bay Lightning
Amalie Arena
401 Channelside Drive
Tampa, FL 33602; 813-301-6500
nhl.com/lightning

236 SOCCER

Orlando City Soccer Club
Inter & Co Stadium
655 West Church Street
Orlando, FL 32805; 855-675-2489
orlandocitysc.com

Of the many springs, 33 are first-magnitude springs discharging an average of 100 cubic feet of water per second. The largest springs channel groundwater from the Florida aquifer, a limestone formation underlying much of the state. Most spring water is at a constant temperature of 68–72°F. Many Florida springs support unique ecosystems and flow into streams and rivers that depend on the influx of freshwater. Springs make wonderful swimming holes and are great places to spot manatees; alligators; otters; and a large variety of fish, birds, and turtles.

Welcome to

SPRINGS

Find out more about SPRINGS

237 ALEXANDER SPRINGS

Alexander Springs Recreational Area
49525 County Road 445
Altoona, FL; 352-669-3522
recreation.gov/camping/campgrounds/234032

Alexander Springs and the recreational area named for it are in the Ocala National Forest, the southernmost and oldest national forest east of the Mississippi River. The recreational area offers camping, swimming, canoeing, scuba diving, hiking, bird-watching, and majestic wildlife viewing. Alexander Springs is among the 33 first-magnitude springs in Florida. (A first-magnitude spring discharges at least 100 cubic feet of water per second.) The clear water is a constant 72°F and has a sandy bottom.

ALEXANDER SPRINGS IS ONE OF THE BEST FOR SWIMMING AND RELAXING, ALTOONA

238 BLUE SPRING STATE PARK

2100 West French Avenue
Orange City, FL 32763; 386-775-3663
floridastateparks.org/parks-and-trails/blue-spring-state-park

This park is a favorite place to watch the West Indian manatee. Hundreds of these gentle animals make Blue Spring their winter home. The spring's constant 72°F temperature also attracts scores of humans enjoying swimming, snorkeling, fishing, and paddling in the clear, unspoiled waters. There are plenty of overlooks and observation points in the park, but it is best to visit the park early in the day to beat the crowds.

239 CRYSTAL RIVER NATIONAL WILDLIFE REFUGE

1502 SE Kings Bay Drive
Crystal River, FL 34429; 352-563-2088
fws.gov/refuge/crystal_river

Crystal River is one of several wildlife refuges in the area managed by the U.S. Fish & Wildlife Service. Located in the last unspoiled and undeveloped spring habitat in Kings Bay, which forms the headwaters of the Crystal River, it is the only refuge created specifically for the protection of the threatened Florida manatee. Nearly 600 manatees spend the winter in Kings Bay. During this season, the most popular manatee-viewing opportunity the refuge offers is from a boardwalk. There are also dozens of commercial ventures in the area that offer guided tours, kayak rentals, and educational opportunities.

240 DE LEON SPRINGS STATE PARK

601 Ponce de Leon Boulevard
De Leon Springs, FL 32130
386-985-4212
floridastateparks.org/parks-and-trails/de-leon-springs-state-park

De Leon Springs State Park is known for its swimming area and restaurant, but the visitor center and other displays are also a rich source of cultural information, looking back 6,000 years into the region's history. Take an eco-history boat tour on which you may see alligators, bald eagles, otters, and wading birds. An unusual and popular feature at the park is the pancake breakfast or lunch at the Old Sugar Mill Pancake House, where you prepare your own pancakes at the table. You can also walk a 4-mile trail through the hardwood forests and cypress swamps and sometimes see wild deer, turkeys, and maybe even a black bear.

241 ICHETUCKNEE SPRINGS STATE PARK

12087 SW US 27
Fort White, FL 32038; 386-497-4690
floridastateparks.org/parks-and-trails/ichetucknee-springs-state-park

Tubing on the Ichetucknee River is a generations-old Florida tradition. The crystal-clear, spring-fed river flows 6 miles through shaded hammocks and wetlands before it joins the Santa Fe River. Most native Floridians know that this river is the real Florida, the way it used to be. It is always cool under the lush tree canopy that shades this river. From the end of May until early September, tubing down the river is the premier activity in the area. You can also picnic, snorkel, canoe, hike, or just chill out.

242 RAINBOW SPRINGS STATE PARK

19158 SW 81st Place Road
Dunnellon, FL 34432; 352-465-8555
floridastateparks.org/parks-and-trails/rainbow-springs-state-park

Rainbow Springs is Florida's fourth-largest spring and forms the headwaters of the Rainbow River. From the 1930s through the 1970s, it was the site of a popular, privately owned attraction and, after closing for several years, reopened as a state park in the 1990s. At the park's main entrance, at the headsprings, you can swim in the freshwater river, rent canoes and kayaks, view waterfalls and gardens, and enjoy a picnic area with grills and pavilions. There are also campsites. Tubes are available farther down the river for floating downstream.

243 SILVER SPRINGS STATE PARK

1425 NE 58th Avenue
Ocala, FL 34470; 352-236-7148
floridastateparks.org/silversprings

For many years, Silver Springs was Florida's most popular commercial tourist attraction. It was famous for its glass-bottom boats and the clarity of the spring-fed Silver River. Many movies were filmed here as well. Lloyd Bridges filmed parts of 100 episodes of the television series *Sea Hunt* here. Over the years, the springs and attraction became a state park. You can still enjoy riding on the glass-bottom boats; paddling in a kayak; or just staring in amazement at the crystal-clear, blue depths of Silver Springs. You can camp here, visit the museum, or eat in the restaurant. Birds and flowers abound, and every now and then a monkey appears, descended from some that escaped from a tour-boat operator who brought them to the area for a Tarzan-themed attraction that never came to fruition.

244 WAKULLA SPRINGS STATE PARK

465 Wakulla Park Drive
Wakulla Springs, FL 32327
850-561-7276
floridastateparks.org/parks-and-trails/edward-ball-wakulla-springs-state-park

The official name of this park is Edward Ball Wakulla Springs State Park, and it is named after the Floridian financier who built a lodge on the property and developed the land as an attraction aimed at preserving wildlife. Many movies were made at these springs, including *Tarzan's Secret Treasure* (1941), starring Johnny Weissmuller. The constant 70°F waters are a wonderful treat on hot summer days. You can also take a 45-minute riverboat tour on which you will usually see alligators, an occasional manatee, and many bird species. You can book a stay at Ball's historic lodge at Wakulla Springs. The magnificence of the lodge alone is worth a trip to this park.

EDWARD BALL WAKULLA SPRINGS ENTRANCE SIGN, WAKULLA SPRINGS

245 WARM MINERAL SPRINGS

12200 San Servando Avenue
North Port, FL 34287; 941-426-1692
Northportfl.gov/Community-Recreation/Parks-Facilities/Warm-Mineral-Springs-Park

Warm Mineral Springs is unique for its year-round temperature of 85°F, much warmer than most Florida springs. It is estimated that the waters contain 51 minerals, one of the highest mineral contents of any natural spring in the United States. The springs have been a public park since 2010, but for many years before that a steady stream of visitors came from around the world for the alleged therapeutic effects of the water. Local legend has it that Ponce de León visited here and that it was the basis for his legendary Fountain of Youth. You can either swim in the water or just sit and soak it up. A variety of spa services, including massages and facials, are also available; call ahead to make a reservation.

246 WEKIWA SPRINGS STATE PARK

1800 Wekiwa Circle
Apopka, FL 32712; 407-553-4383
floridastateparks.org/parks-and-trails/wekiwa-springs-state-park

Wekiwa Springs has been a popular recreational spot for Orlando-area residents and tourists for more than 100 years. It is so popular that on many days from May through October they have to close it when the maximum capacity of 250 cars has been reached. The clear, cool springs feed the Wekiwa River, and in addition to a large swimming area, there are miles of trails for hiking, biking, or horseback riding. Canoes and kayaks can be rented in the park, and you can paddle along the Wekiwa River and Rock Springs Run. A full-facility campground is also located in a quiet section of the park.

Springs in Florida are popular places for cooling off while scuba diving, swimming, or observing the multitude of animals that also enjoy the fresh, cool water.

A CLOSE-UP SHOT OF A MALAYAN TIGER AT ZOO TAMPA AT LOWRY PARK, TAMPA

Florida is known for having world-class attractions, and its zoos are no exception.

They are home to animals native to the state but are also populated with many other species from all over the world. Some Florida animals you will see are panthers, alligators, snakes, foxes, frogs, and a wide variety of birds. Some zoos may have elephants, giraffes, anteaters, bears, Gila monsters, and manatees. Many Florida zoos have up-close animal encounters that kids especially love, and in some cases you are allowed to feed certain animals.

Welcome to

ZOOS

Find out more about ZOOS

247 BREVARD ZOO

8225 North Wickham Road
Melbourne, FL 32940; 321-254-9453
brevardzoo.org

The small Brevard Zoo is one of the most popular zoos in Florida. You will see more than 195 species that include more than 900 different animals creatively housed on restored wetlands. The animals originate from Florida, Asia, Africa, Australia, and South America. One of the features of this zoo is that you can feed animals, such as the giraffes and birds, and you can ride a miniature train around the grounds through the animal's natural habitat. You can also purchase special tickets at the zoo that give you a unique adventure, such as paddling a kayak or enjoying the petting zoo.

248 CATTY SHACK RANCH WILDLIFE SANCTUARY

1860 Starratt Road
Jacksonville, FL 32226; 904-757-3603
cattyshack.org

Catty Shack Ranch is a nonprofit wildlife sanctuary in Jacksonville. It has become one of the area's most popular visitor attractions. Their primary mission is to give endangered big cats a permanent home. They specialize in the rescue of exotic animals that are in danger. When an animal arrives at Catty Shack Ranch, it will have a loving home for the rest of its life. None of these animals are used for breeding, trading, selling, or buying. Animals currently living at Catty Shack Ranch include tigers, lions, leopards, lynxes, foxes, and coati. Even though the last two aren't cats, they have been given "honorary cat" status by the ranch.

249 GATORLAND

14501 South Orange Blossom Trail
Orlando, FL 32837; 407-855-5496
gatorland.com

Gatorland has been thrilling visitors since 1949, a full 22 years before neighboring Walt Disney World opened its doors. It is a place for family fun, and the 110-acre park offers a true glimpse into the Old Florida that is so quickly disappearing. You will see thousands of alligators (including some white ones), some crocodiles, a free-flight aviary, and several animal shows. For an extra charge, you can even soar above the hungry gators on a zip line.

250 JACKSONVILLE ZOO AND GARDENS

370 Zoo Parkway
Jacksonville, FL 32218; 904-757-4463
jacksonvillezoo.org

This zoo is more than 100 years old and is located on 122 acres on the shore of Trout River, north of downtown Jacksonville. The zoo is organized by natural exhibits, including River Valley Aviary, African Forest, Stingray Bay, Wild Florida, Giraffe Overlook, and Range of the Jaguar. For the kids, there is also the Play Park and Splash Ground and the ability to pet the stingrays in Stingray Bay. The Gardens at Trout River Plaza is a large botanical garden where facilities can be rented for special events. Kids also love feeding the lorikeets at Australian Adventure.

251 LION COUNTRY SAFARI

2003 Lion Country Safari Road
Loxahatchee, FL 33470; 561-793-1084
lioncountrysafari.com

Lion Country Safari is an unusual amusement park where you drive your own car through the grounds to view more than 1,000 animals. The attraction also has rides and a water-spray feature for the kids, animal-feeding experiences, a restaurant, shops, a campground, and a lot more. Some of the animals you will see include tortoises, tapirs, alpacas, impalas, ostriches, water buffaloes, lions, Ankole-Watusi cattle, rhinos, zebras, and chimpanzees.

252 NAPLES ZOO AT CARIBBEAN GARDENS

1590 Goodlette-Frank Road
Naples, FL 34102; 239-262-5409
napleszoo.org

This zoo was established in 1919, when Naples was still a small settlement. It was originally a botanical garden, which explains its full name. Many of the more than 3,000 plants from the original gardens are still thriving today. Animals live in habitats designed to enhance their freedom and natural surroundings. You will see gators, anteaters, bears, cheetahs, snakes, foxes, frogs, gibbons, and even a honey badger that the children love to interact with (he's behind very strong glass).

253 ST. AUGUSTINE ALLIGATOR FARM ZOOLOGICAL PARK

999 Anastasia Boulevard
St. Augustine, FL 32080
904-824-3337
alligatorfarm.com

This is one of several Floridian tourist attractions on the National Register of Historic Places. It was founded in 1893 and has entertained and educated millions of people about alligators. This zoo also has hundreds of other species, including birds, lemurs, snakes, turtles, and even porcupines and albino alligators. The attraction also has a zip line where you can soar over the gators as you imagine them licking their chops.

254 ZOO TAMPA AT LOWRY PARK

1101 West Sligh Avenue
Tampa, FL 33604; 813-935-8552
zootampa.org

This zoo is one of the most popular in Florida, with over 1 million annual visitors. The zoo occupies 56 acres with numerous animal exhibits and has many up-close animal encounters that both kids and adults enjoy. The zoo pays special attention to endangered species from world climates similar to that of the Tampa Bay area. The park has areas devoted to Asia, Africa, Australia, and Florida. More than 1,300 animals make their home in the zoo. Another interesting feature is the Manatee Critical Care Center, the only one of its kind in Florida. Stingray Shores gives you a chance to feed and pet the stingrays.

255 ZOO WORLD

9008 Front Beach Road
Panama City Beach, FL 32407
850-230-1243
zooworldpcb.com

This zoo specializes in conservation and has over 260 animals with numerous exhibits, programs, and performances in a tropical setting. At this interactive attraction, you can have up-close experiences with sloths, giraffes, lemurs, alligators, and birds. These encounters usually include holding and petting the animal. Most of the encounters cost an additional fee. There are also various dispensers around the zoo where you can buy food to feed the animals.

INDEX

PHOTO CREDITS

Photos by Mike Miller except as follows:

Bonnie Whicher: 147

These images are used under Attribution 2.0 Generic (CC BY 2.0) license, which can be found at https://creativecommons.org/licenses/by/2.0/: **B A Bowen Photography:** 98, no modifications, original image at flickr.com/photos/riverbk/4088720212/; **Bob B. Brown:** 103, no modifications, original image at flickr.com/photos/beleaveme/7994309805/; **Charles:** 92 (Revs Institute), no modifications, original image at flickr.com/photos/charles79/52338834371/; **Rusty Clark ~ 100K Photos:** 50, no modifications, original image at flickr.com/photos/rusty_clark/9652419505/, 55, no modifications, original image at flickr.com/photos/rusty_clark/6691626895/; **Anna Fox:** 9, no modifications, original image at flickr.com/photos/harshlight/5302134835/; **Steven Miller:** 68, no modifications, original image at flickr.com/photos/aloha75/13682347865/; **Infrogmation of New Orleans:** 119, no modifications, original image at flickr.com/photos/infrogmation/4723404424/; **Jared:** 95, no modifications, original image at flickr.com/photos/jared422/15732705498/, 97, no modifications, original image at flickr.com/photos/jared422/7213582528/; **David Moore:** 45 (Smallwood Store), no modifications, original image at flickr.com/photos/55647737@N04/50521623158/; **Robin Wendell:** 4 (Weeki Wachee mermaid), no modifications, original image at flickr.com/photos/130946855@N03/15761430853/;

This image is used under Attribution 3.0 (CC BY 3.0) license, which can be found at https://creativecommons.org/licenses/by/3.0/us/deed.en: **Averette:** 83, no modifications, original image at https-:commons.wikimedia.org:w:index.php?curid=4267842.tif

All images used under license from Shutterstock.com:
absolute Illustration: 4 (big top); **aceshot1:** 62; **A Cotton Photo:** 107; **AHPix:** 90; **anderm:** xii (Cape Florida light); **Andre-Johnson:** 101; **Andrewaarons:** 8; **Andrew Angelov:** 126; **Brittany De Armas:** 64 (Schnebly Redland's Winery); **Barks:** 133; **Bonnie Taylor Barry:** 18; **Martina Birnbaum:** 34; **Varina C:** 104; **Kolben Clayton:** 57; **Estelle Cress:** 130; **cve iv:** 121; **Thierry Eidenweil:** 20; **Low Flite:** 58; **Fotogro:** 84; **Nick Fox:** 132; **Zack Frank:** 45 (Shark Valley Observation Tower); **GagliardiPhotography:** i (everglades); **Graphicyes:** 22 (dolphin); **Irina Gutyryak:** i (asphalt); **HDP Digital:** 110; **Margarita Hintukainen:** 1 (Fruit & Spice Park); **Infinity Moments LLC:** 2; **IrinaK:** 40, 108; **JB Studio Design:** 125; **Mariusz S. Jurgielewicz:** 12 (The Ringling Museum of Art); **Leo Kavalli:** 89; **KristinBSmith:** 6; **Cynthia Liang:** 32; **majic-photos:** 78; **MaK999:** 75; **LaurenAnnGraham:** 116; **L Paul Mann:** 46; **Margaret.Wiktor:** 16; **Billy McDonald:** 56; **Valerijs Novickis:** i (Ginnie Springs); **Timothy OLeary:** 128; **Ografica:** 64 (Spanish food); **Samuel Parsons:** 112; **PeskyMonkey:** 10; **photo.eccles:** 39; **Real_life_photo:** 26; **Mathew Risley:** 81; **SandyShusterPhotography:** 122; **Galina Savina:** 70; **Jim Schwabel:** 1 (anhinga); **Sharon Davies Photography:** 22 (gulf fritillary); **Barbara Smyers:** 52; **summer studio:** 115; **swarnstudio:** 109; **Erin Westgate:** 102; **Melissa L White:** 7; **Wirestock Creators:** 134; **wittyvectors:** 92 (air conditioner); **Olga Yaroshenko:** 12 (paint palette); **Zulfihakim:** 72

ABOUT THE AUTHOR

Mike Miller is a blogger, writer, consulting engineer, and speaker who has lived in Florida for most of his life. He owns the popular website FloridaBackroadsTravel.com and is the author of 18 books about the Sunshine State. His writing focuses on Florida off the beaten path and tells readers about the rich Floridian history that informs their travel. He has driven an estimated 2 million miles in Florida in too many cars to count and has sailed all of Florida's coasts and Keys in sailboats. Mike received a BS in Civil Engineering from the University of Florida and is a registered professional engineer and licensed real estate broker. He served in the U.S. Navy, owned his own consulting engineering firm, and had key roles in the construction of Walt Disney World, EPCOT, and Universal Studios Florida. He loves to write and speak about his home state.

Florida Day Trips celebrates Florida's unique nature and reflects Mike's lifetime of exploring the Sunshine State.

The Story of AdventureKEEN

We are an independent nature and outdoor activity publisher. Our founding dates back more than 40 years, guided then and now by our love of being in the woods and on the water, by our passion for reading and books, and by the sense of wonder and discovery made possible by spending time recreating outdoors in beautiful places.

It is our mission to share that wonder and fun with our readers, especially with those who haven't yet experienced all the physical and mental health benefits that nature and outdoor activity can bring.

In addition, we strive to teach about responsible recreation so that the natural resources and habitats we cherish and rely upon will be available for future generations.

We are a small team deeply rooted in the places where we live and work. We have been shaped by our communities of origin—primarily Birmingham, Alabama; Cincinnati, Ohio; and the northern suburbs of Minneapolis, Minnesota. Drawing on the decades of experience of our staff and our awareness of the industry, the marketplace, and the world at large, we have shaped a unique vision and mission for a company that serves our readers and authors.

We hope to meet you out on the trail someday.

#bewellbeoutdoors